Sport Science Secrets:
from myth to facts

Gordon W. Russell

Printed in Victoria, Canada

National Library of Canada Cataloguing in Publication Data

Russell, Gordon W., 1931-
 Sport science secrets

 Includes bibliographical references.
 ISBN 1-55212-638-2

 1. Sports sciences. I. Title.
GV558.R87 2001   796'.01'5   C2001-910403-0

TRAFFORD

This book was published *on-demand* in cooperation with Trafford Publishing.
On-demand publishing is a unique process and service of making a book available for retail sale to the public taking advantage of on-demand manufacturing and Internet marketing.
On-demand publishing includes promotions, retail sales, manufacturing, order fulfilment, accounting and collecting royalties on behalf of the author.

Suite 6E, 2333 Government St., Victoria, B.C. V8T 4P4, CANADA
Phone   250-383-6864   Toll-free   1-888-232-4444 (Canada & US)
Fax   250-383-6804   E-mail   sales@trafford.com
Web site   www.trafford.com   TRAFFORD PUBLISHING IS A DIVISION OF TRAFFORD HOLDINGS LTD.
Trafford Catalogue #01-0040   www.trafford.com/robots/01-0040.html

10   9   8   7   6   5

Dedicated to my granddaughter:

Serena Dawn Svidal

TABLE OF CONTENTS

IV. TIPS ON IMPROVING PERFORMANCE

V. THE DECISION MAKERS

VI. MYTHS SURROUNDING SPORTS

X. RISKS, HEALTH AND SPORTS

XI. MEDIA AND THE BUSINESS OF SPORTS

XII. THE FACE OF VIOLENCE: SOME NEW WRINKLES

PREFACE

The central part played by sports in the lives of Americans is seen in the results of a national poll done in 1986. Fully 71% of the adult population identified themselves as sports fans while 73% indicated that they were currently participating in a sport or recreational activity. For most, sports are much more than a passing interest suggesting instead that they hold our attention and interest for a significant portion of each waking day. As we will see later on these pages, sports can also influence our emotional states, shape our attitudes/behaviors and affect how we view the world around us.

Media observers and critics are fond of telling us that news coverage -- especially television -- is at best superficial. Numerous events occurring world-wide compete for a place in the 30 minutes allotted to the evening news. On a slow day, an environmental disaster in Brazil may be the lead story. On a day when news of a major world event(s) is flashed across the airwaves, the Brazilian story is apt to be pushed to the sidelines and perhaps, not even appear on our screens. Thus, the depth of coverage and importance given to a story is very much dependent upon the fickle behavior of broadcasting executives in juggling newsworthy stories and time slots. What we as media consumers ultimately get are bare-boned, factual summaries of events as they are known to reporters at the time. For most of us, these news bytes provide all of the basic information we need to get a clear overview of the story.

There is an obvious parallel between the evening news and this book. The essential facts representing what we presently know about over one hundred fascinating sports topics and issues are presented in a condensed form in a book I have titled *Sport Science Secrets: From Myth to Facts.* My goal was to discuss the topics with sufficient clarity and detail to satisfy the curiosity of 99% of my readers.

Sport Science Secrets is intended to put the reader in direct contact with the work of those who have the inside track on human behavior in sports. Countless researchers in fields such as sociology, psychology, physical education, medicine and economics have invested their time and energies investigating behavior in the sports world. The targets of these investigations included athletes, fans, officials, the sports media and those in management. The work of these researchers generally appears in scientific journals primarily intended for an audience of their peers. There the information rests except as some of it trickles down to the general public through textbooks, lectures and the occasional media interview. I would like to help bridge the gap between academia and those who share my interest and love of sports. *Sport Science Secrets* then is my attempt to provide the average sports enthusiast with a reader-friendly, entertaining and informative overview of intriguing and often controversial topics from the sports world.

The focus of my efforts in preparing the topics has been to distill the writings of my scientific colleagues to just those findings that interest the average sports fan. Equally important, I have tried to present the often heady writings of my colleagues in everyday language. This by the way was my stiffest challenge, trying to walk that fine line between recasting the specialized jargon of scientists into everyday language at the same time doing justice to their work. Admittedly, I sometimes erred on the side of too much jargon; at other times I oversimplified matters.

And now, a word about the research that underlies each of the 103 chapters. At the outset, it is important to recognise that the quality of the research cited varies widely. The fact of a paper being published in a journal in no way guarantees that it is without flaws. Some studies are poorly designed, often lacking sufficient controls and adequate sampling procedures. Moreover, some of the chapters are based on only a single study whereas other topics have been investigated by literally dozens of researchers. Where an extensive literature underlies a chapter, I have cited several sport-relevant articles that in my humble opinion reflect current thinking on the topic. No attempt has been made to provide an exhaustive literature review in such cases. However, related readings are provided in the references for those readers/students wishing to explore a topic in greater depth.

To conclude, I should mention that the topics I have chosen are not a random selection by any means. Particular care was taken specifically to choose topics that challenge common assumptions, dispel myths, correct misinformation or offer fresh ways of thinking about our behavior in the world of sports. I think that many of the chapters will surprise you. So, if you are occasionally surprised and at the same time feel better informed and entertained, then I will have achieved my purpose.

I. Individual Performance

Introduction:

The common thread in this opening section is an emphasis on differences among individuals that affect their progress/development in a sport. In addition to a comparison of competition and cooperation, the chapters also highlight the relationships between athletes' performance and their physical characteristics, for example, race, age, eye color, handedness. Two additional chapters emphasize the role of the athlete's motivation and the age at which athletes peak.

1 Competition: Not All It's Cracked Up to be

Perhaps the most central and hallowed concept in the sportsworld is "competition". However, sportspeople are not alone in paying homage to the term. We also see it as the preferred means of interacting with others in the business and scientific communities. Because of its widespread acceptance, particularly in North America, one might be forgiven for concluding that when our interactions are conducted in a spirit of competition, it draws the best performances from people. That is, compared to cooperation or an individualistic approach, competition is thought to bring out the very best in us.

To ensure that we are using competition in the same way, allow me to offer a definition of the term, i.e., "...two or more units, either individuals or groups, engaged in pursuing the same rewards, with these rewards so defined that if they are attained by any one unit, there are fewer rewards for the other units in the situation" (Berkowitz, 1962, p. 178). Thus, unlike cooperation where everyone stands to win something, competition dictates that one person's winnings are another person's losses. There is only one winner of the 100m dash, the Superbowl or a boxing match, the others in the field are "also rans" or, "losers".

Considering the importance that attaches to the assumed relationship between competition and superior performance, it is not surprising that social scientists have carried out numerous studies directly comparing competition to cooperation. When 109 such analyses were combined to provide an overview on the question, 65 showed cooperation to be a superior means of interacting, 36 showed no advantage to either style and only 8 favored competition.

How important is cooperation relative to competition in the real world? When we look at a number of occupations we see clearly that competition is not generally associated with success. What does appear to contribute to achieving success is a combination of, (1) a preference for challenging and difficult tasks plus, (2) the enjoyment of hard work plus, (3) low competitiveness. This combination has been shown to predict success among PhDs in biology, engineering and psychology. Moreover, it is also related to higher salaries among businessmen and higher grade point averages among male and female college students.

Do men and women differ in their preferences for competitive vs. cooperative styles of interacting with people? Indeed, they differ sharply. Females exhibit a strong preference for activities that are conducted along cooperative lines. By contrast, men are highly competitive in their day to day dealings. By all available evidence, it seems that women may have it right.

The message that comes through is clear. It is time for us to re-evaluate our emphasis in North America on competition and consider redirecting our energies to focus more on activities for youngsters that encourage cooperative attitudes and behaviors. It just might put the fun back into sports and games. After all, fun is what childhood is supposed to be all about.

2 Handicapped By your Birthdate

"...not tonight dear, it's too early in the year"

At the time when nearly all of us started school in grade 1, many of us also started baseball, ice hockey or soccer. To avoid the chaos that would result if parents could choose the date for enrolling their children, sports organizations simply set the date by which the youngster must have reached, for example, their sixth birthday. Children turning six after the deadline must in most cases wait almost an entire year before beginning their sports "careers".

The best available evidence on this question, called the "relative age effect" is to be found in the research program of a team of Canadian researchers. They carefully recorded the birthdates of seasoned athletes from several major

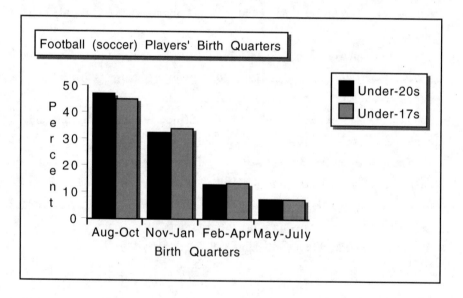

sports and arranged them according to the months of the year. As we see in the Figure (adapted from Barnsley et al., 1992) of Under-20, most world class players had birthdates just after the traditional deadline, i.e., August 1, for initially enrolling in soccer programs when they were children. A mere 8% had birthdates in the May-July quarter just before the deadline. The Figure further shows that in the case of Under-17s soccer players the frequency of birthdates again exhibits the same dramatic drop from the Aug-Oct quarter to the May-July quarter. Essentially the same pattern of results have been found in baseball, football and ice hockey. It thus becomes clear that what happens to a 5 or 6-year old at the registration desk can dramatically determine their success in a sport all the way through to adulthood, 15 or more years later.

These sorts of organizational rules would seem necessary if officials of a sport are to administer a program in an even-handed and fair manner. Yet, the imposition of a deadline unfortunately produces a situation that is anything but fair and one that works against the development of talent in a sport.

The unfairness lies with the arbitrary deadline, say January 1st for having reached your next birthday. Children born late in the calendar year who squeeze into a program just before the deadline find themselves playing alongside peers who are almost a year older. This occurs during a period of rapid social and physical development. Consequently, the teammates of late born children generally are more physically and emotionally mature, and have better developed social skills. Clearly, late born youngsters are at a disadvantage even before they begin. But surely they can catch up. So, where is the problem? The problem is that most don't catch up and either leave their sport or struggle through unimpressive careers.

The relative age effect presents an exceedingly bothersome problem for officials in a number of youth sports. Beyond a recognition that later borns face particular difficulties in competing alongside better coordinated, stronger and more socially adept peers, it has been suggested that we postpone the formation of all-star teams. These are usually made up of early-borns in an age category and only serve to widen the gap in abilities that already exists. Ability grouping, encouragement and/or special coaching for later-borns may also minimize differences in the development of their native talents.

Incidentally, if parenthood is in your future, you might give some thought to your child's age vis-a-vis his/her maturity when school registration time rolls around. It may be one of the most important decisions you will ever make on behalf of your youngster. That is to say, the relative age effect is just as clearly in evidence in the school system as it is in sports.

As a footnote, allow me to draw your attention to a further study that underlines the critical importance of the relative age effect in peoples' lives. A recent finding shows a strong link to teenage suicide. The study was based on 564 young people under the age of 20 who had taken their lives. Those born in the second half of the "school eligibility year" had a higher probability of a completed suicide.

3 Age and Peak Performance

Over nearly the entire span of Olympic history the age of gold medalists has remained remarkably constant. For example, winners of the 1500-meter run from 1896 to 1986 averaged 25 years of age as they did for the period 1948 to 1980. Other events listed in Table 1 showed a similar pattern of consistency of age over time.

An examination of the Table (below) shows a strong trend in the track events. As the length of the events increase from 100-meters to the 50 km walk, there is a corresponding increase in the average ages of gold medalists, a trend that is also apparent for women. Also evident in the case of swimming are gender differences. The average age of female medalists was approximately 18 years of age, that of men 20 years.

The records of the United States Tennis Association provided the ages at which men and women achieved a No. 1 world ranking. From 1885 to 1978 the average age of men ranked No. 1 was 25. Women who achieved the top spot in world tennis from 1913 to 1975 was 23. Golfers peak much later. The performance of Professional Golf Association players in recent years has peaked around 31 years of age. However, there is also evidence that the age of peak golfing performance has been gradually declining.

Table 1.

Peak Performance and Age: Olympic Gold Medalists (1896-1980).

	Age	
	Men	Women
Events		
Track and field:		
100-meter	23	21
200-meter	24	22
800-meter	24	24
1500-meter	25	~
5000-meter	27	~
10,000-meter	28	~
marathon	28	~
50 km walk	29	~
Other:		
long jump	23	24
high jump	23	23
shot put	24	26
Swimming:		
100-meter freestyle	21	19
400-meter freestyle	20	18
800-meter freestyle	~	16
1500-meter freestyle	20	~

adapted from Schultz & Curnow (1988)

The records of major league baseball have also been used to establish the age of peak performance for a number of categories. Taking the amount of playing time as an indication of players' overall playing abilities, we see the number of starts for hitters and pitchers peak at age 27. With few exceptions, we again find

27 to be the age of peak performance when players' lifetime performance records are examined. However, among hitters the percentage of walks and fielding average peaks a little later, around age 30. Two key measures of pitching ability, i.e., number of wins and earned run average, also peak later, around 29.

The age profile of Hall of Famers reveals a somewhat different pattern than that of other slightly less talented major league players. While they were superior at an earlier age, both hitters and pitchers reached their peak at a later age than their teammates and indeed, maintained their superior play for a longer period of time.

Bear in mind that all of the above figures are averages. In every performance category some athletes are much younger, others, much older. Lou Brock stole 118 bases at age 34; the average is 27 years. Need I remind anyone that golfer, Tiger Woods is 24 while Sergio Garcia is 20, the average being 31. Take heart. There is always the seniors tour!

4 Eye Color and Racial Differences in Performance

The sports fraternity has long recognized racial differences in athletic performance. Although the underlying explanations for these differences vary, certain sports or skills appear to favor one race over another. Whether for reasons of restricted access to a sport, different socialization experiences or, the greater attraction of some sports over others, Black and White athletes have been shown to differ in their performance of certain skills. The reference here is not simply to the everyday observation that Blacks are overly represented in boxing and at the same time rarely seen on the professional golf tour. These imbalances obviously occur for some of the reasons noted above. What is more central to answering questions of racial differences in performance are comparisons in a sport(s) that offers relatively equal access to aspiring athletes of either race.

One of the early suggestions was that Black athletes excel at **reactive** sports or activities. Thus, skills such as batting (baseball) and field goal shooting (basketball) where the athlete is required to respond to quickly changing circumstances at times dictated by others, were thought to favor Blacks. By contrast, activities that are **self-paced**, where the athlete responds at a time of his/her own choosing in a fairly unchanging situation, were thought to favor White athletes. Pitching in baseball and free-throws in basketball are good examples of self-paced activities.

An interesting complication was added to the original distinction between reactive and self-paced activities, namely, eye color. The claim was made that dark-eyed people will be superior at reactive activities that require speed and quick reactions. Light-eyed persons were thought to be better at self-paced activities where speed and fast reactions were less important. As an example, a clear prediction from baseball would be that Blacks would excel at batting whereas Whites would excel at pitching.

The claims regarding eye color were far from being idle speculation. Evidence from other species in the animal kingdom reveal among other things, that dark-eyed birds have faster flying speeds than light-eyed birds. Similarly, birds of prey are generally darker-eyed in contrast to seed eaters. Even the lowly fruitfly exhibits the same pattern with the dark-eyed version being speedier. However, it is a considerable reach to extend these observations to the ball diamond and basketball court.

How do these ideas regarding eye-color and type of activity play out when they are tested against the official records of professional baseball and basketball? For starters, it appeared at the time of the first study (1970) that Blacks were overrepresented among hitters and underrepresented on the mound. This same study also found that while Black (dark-eyed) basketball players had marginally better field goal performances, White players were clearly superior at the free throw line. In the second 1973 study Black and White players were found to be equally accurate from the field. However, Whites again demonstrated superior free-throw statistics. In an analysis that indeed confirms that "white men can't jump", Black basketball players were found to be better rebounders. And finally, let's hear it for the little guys! Shorter players, regardless of race, were more accurate at the free throw line than their taller teammates.

An examination of racial differences in baseball show Blacks (dark-eyed) to be clearly superior at the plate. Various measures of hitting skills reveal that blacks score more runs, get more hits and home runs and, have higher batting averages than their White teammates.

The story is much the same when we look to pitching. Although Whites were predicted to be superior on the mound, a self-paced activity, just the opposite seems to be the case. Black pitchers have more strikeouts, win more games, give up fewer hits and have higher winning percentages. However, the authors point out that their sample of Black pitchers was small. Moreover, given the barriers facing Black pitchers at that time, it may be that only those who were truly exceptional made it to the major leagues. Not surprisingly, a refined group of "exceptional" Black pitchers would outperform a group comprised of both exceptional and average White hurlers.

Overall, it must be said that the proposed racial links to reactive vs. self-paced activities has found only weak support in studies. The eye-color hypothesis, intertwined with race, has found even less support. While it may be the case that eye color, independent of race, is predictive of some sport performances, convincing evidence to that effect has yet to surface. Nevertheless, reaction times have been shown to be marginally different for dark and light-eyed people. Dark-eyed subjects responded more quickly in a simple reaction time task than did those with light colored eyes. Females too have shown themselves to have faster reaction times than males. If there is merit to be found in eye-color hypotheses, it is more apt to be found in sports such as fencing, badminton or ping pong where fast reactions are the key to success.

5 White Men Can't Jump: Black Men Can't Swim

Drowning is the second most common cause of unintentional injury death for people between the ages of 5 and 44 years. Safety figures also reveal a striking difference in rates of drowning between Blacks and Whites. Not only are Blacks 2 to 3 times more likely to be victims of drowning but they are also underrepresented in competitive swimming and occupations requiring swimming skills. Correct me if I am wrong on this but US Olympic swim teams have yet to include a Black athlete.

A variety of explanations have been advanced to explain the differences in swimming ability. At a physiological level, Blacks generally have less subcutaneous fat and denser bones that reduces buoyancy and makes learning strokes more difficult. Social explanations highlight the lack of swimming facilities and opportunities available to Blacks. Similarly, summer camps and the Boy Scouts where swimming skills are emphasized, may be less a part of the Black experience.

A large scale study of over 2,500 West Point cadets sought to examine the importance of these and numerous other factors that might influence swimming ability. Easily the strongest factor for Blacks and Whites was the age at which the cadets had first learned to swim. Those who learned at an early age were among the better swimmers in the cadet corps. By age 9, over 90% of Whites had learned to swim in contrast to 58% of Blacks. Across all ages, Black swimmers were less skillful than White swimmers.

Matters of buoyancy and bone density did not appear to affect swimming ability. Rather, factors such as watching less television and not having earlier part-time work as youngsters was related to Blacks becoming better swimmers. Interestingly, whereas White females learned to swim earlier than White males, just the opposite was true of the Black cadets. That is, Black women began swimming at a later age than Black men. Faced with this puzzling reversal, the authors offer an intriguing explanation based on racial differences in hair texture.

Apparently, the styling of Blacks' hair after swimming is much more time consuming and makes even recreational swimming a less attractive activity to Black women (whatever happened to bathing caps?).

6 Batting Right Versus Batting Left

What do we know about the performance of baseball players who bat from the right side of the plate and others who hit from the left side? Also, do right-handed players differ from left-handed players in their performance at the plate? The answers to these questions were found in the historical record. That is, the batting performance of all players competing in Major League Baseball from its inception in 1871 to 1992 was analyzed. First, the results overall strongly favored left-handers over right-handed players *regardless of which side of the plate they hit from*. Lefties were superior in:

◆ batting average
◆ home runs
◆ bases on balls
◆ slugging average (an index of power hitting based on the number
   of bases a batter reaches on average for each time at bat)

The two groups did not differ in strikeouts and stolen bases.

Turning now to a comparison of batters who hit right versus those who hit from the left side of the plate *regardless of their hand preference*. Those batting from the left side exhibit clearly superior batting skills. They easily surpass those hitting from the right side in:

◆ batting average
◆ home runs
◆ bases on balls
◆ slugging average
◆ (fewer) strikeouts

Only the number of stolen bases did not differ between the two groups.

The records of the Major League Baseball Hall of Fame further attest to the greater success of players who have batted left. Of the 111 hitters in the Hall of Fame (not including switch-hitters) 54 hit left, a figure out of all proportion to the number of lefties in organized baseball.

Now we focus on differences in batting preference between left and right-handed players who *hit from the left side* of the plate (a substantial number of right-handed players choose to bat left). Lefties excelled at power hitting. They had a higher slugging average and hit more home runs than right-handed players. At last something positive to report about right-handers at the plate. When batting from the left side, right-handers had fewer strikeouts. To summarize, when batting from the left side of the plate lefties excel at power hitting but at the same time they strike out more often.

A concluding finding reported in this study is worth noting and involves the relationships between the physical size of ball players and their performance at the plate. Taking *all* players into account, taller players had a generally higher number of home runs and higher slugging averages. The same is true of heavier players. However, both taller and heavier players struck out more often.

7 Two Types of Motivation

What motivates us to do the things we do? What prompts the choice of a particular sport or activity from among all those that are available? What causes some people to drop out of a sport while others persist? These are fundamental questions that go to the heart of human behavior. Although there are numerous theories that offer insights into motivation, one in particular stands out in highlighting a misplaced emphasis in sports. What we see are practices that have the unintended effect of undermining performance in the very sports they were designed to help.

Recent years have seen the development of a major theory of motivation, **Cognitive Evaluation theory**. During this same period, social scientists have found strong evidence in support of predictions made by the theory. At the outset, we should distinguish between two types of motivation, intrinsic and extrinsic. To quote the authors, intrinsic motivation "...is the innate, natural propensity to engage one's interests and exercise one's capacities, and in so doing, to seek and conquer optimal challenges" (Deci & Ryan, 1985, p. 43). Thus, intrinsic motivation is a motivational force that arises spontaneously within all of us. It is sufficient to foster learning, intellectual development and is seen to underlay the acquisition of skills throughout our lifetimes.

People take up and persist at activities solely on the basis of the joy and feelings of personal satisfaction that the activities provide. Consider if you will, the legions of unpaid volunteers who are the lifeblood of many sports, those who enjoy gardening or others who like to fly kites or hike in the mountains. Their satisfactions are personal and largely internal. Of course, among those participating in organized sports, many also pursue their favorite event on the basis of intrinsic motivation. However, intrinsic motivation is all too easily eroded by a host of extrinsic factors that surround sports.

The most obvious extrinsic factor that is seen in organized sports is money. A financial payoff for engaging in an activity appears to affect us in two ways. Assuming that the activity is one we find interesting to begin with, people who are paid now find it less enjoyable and additionally, express less interest in continuing with the activity in the future.

Of course, financial incentives are not alone in reducing intrinsic motivation. Athletes whose efforts meet with any degree of success in a sport are soon showered with awards, ribbons, trophies, prizes and publicity, a practice that potentially weakens intrinsic motivation. Moreover, when one is engaged in an optimally challenging activity, the presence of spectators can similarly undermine intrinsic motivation. Just as important, the presence of a knowledgeable audience can also lead to a less creative performance. In sports such as figure skating, synchronized swimming and rhythmic gymnastics where artistic expression largely defines success, the implications are straightforward.

Finally, recognition should also be taken of the negative impact of rivalry on intrinsically motivated athletes. Rivalry is an all too common attitude that sees the athlete believing that the object of a competition is that of defeating, hurting or in some way beating an opponent. Others compete with the view of doing well against some personal standard of excellence; winning is not necessarily all that important. Where rivalry prevails, we see a decrease in intrinsic motivation, a decrease that is even greater among female athletes.

The question that I have yet to explain is why money, trophies, publicity and spectators should reduce a motivational basis for performing tasks that we find interesting. The theorists suggest that the presence of external factors can cause people to undergo a change from an internal to an external locus of causality. That is, intrinsic motivation arises from a basic human need to be **self-determining**. When external factors are present, it becomes difficult for a person to maintain self-determination. Rewards can become ends in themselves. Doubts arise and what was previously done for the challenge and inherent interest it provided is now more likely to be undertaken for externally-based reasons.

Thus, instead of performing simply for the joy and satisfaction that sports provide, athletes gradually come to believe that they are competing for trophies, titles, money, publicity or the approval of spectators. From the point of view of the theory, this shift in focus to external reasons for their participation can result in an athlete losing interest and/or performing less well, among other things.

Curiously, the more an athlete achieves in a sport, the more extrinsic incentives are provided. These "fruits of success" in turn, undermine intrinsic motivation, the very type of motivation that allowed the athlete to reach his/her present, high standard of performance. I would like to think that sports can still be played just for fun. My own guess is that youngsters playing a pick-up game of baseball, soccer or basketball probably have more fun and learn more valuable lessons than they do in an "organized" version of their sport. Perhaps, adults should occasionally resist the urge to organize a league, get sponsors and find monies for uniforms, trophies, trips, and end-of-season banquets. The greatest rewards can be just in the play itself.

Summary

This opening section highlighted a variety of factors that underlie the success of individual athletic performance. We began with the well-researched topic of competition in a chapter that challenges a sacred assumption and which may have been unsettling for some readers, reassuring for others. Some factors, e.g., date of birth, age, race, handedness, are givens while others, e.g., one's competitive vs. cooperative attitudes, an intrinsic vs. extrinsic motivation, are somewhat flexible and can be modified. However, an individual approach is only part of the story.

II. Team Performance

Introduction

We turn now to a set of chapters that consider athletic performance mainly at the team level. Teams playing at home in many sports enjoy some measure of advantage. Of particular interest are the numerous reasons found to underlie that performance edge. We will also see in Chapter 11 that the numbers "just don't add up" in team play. Is it conceivable that the traditional Olympic powerhouses, for example, Germany, USA and USSR have been overtaken by a tiny African nation? Finally, why is it that our strongest supporters may sometimes bring about our downfall?

8 The Home Field Advantage

It is commonly recognized that teams playing at home enjoy a performance advantage over visiting opponents. The belief has received consistent and widespread support from social scientists. There are however, a number of points worth noting about the home field advantage. First of all, the phenomenon is not new. It can be found in English First Division soccer records dating back to the latter part of the 19th century. There is a further suggestion that the margin of advantage was even greater in days past. Note should also be taken of the fact that the home field advantage varies in size from sport to sport. While playing at home provides a sizable advantage in sports such as soccer, ice hockey and basketball, it is less pronounced in football and, provides only a slight edge to baseball teams. However, the really intriguing question surrounding this topic has to do with "why".

What exactly gives athletes playing at home an edge over their visitors? A popular explanation and one that I want to dispel is the suggestion that it derives from athletes being more proficient in defense of their own turf or "territory". The notion of territoriality originates with the ethological research tradition of observing lower animals in their natural surroundings. Certainly, it is a useful concept for explaining the behaviors of some animals. It is worth noting in this regard that only some animals in fact establish territories. In fact, not all herd animals establish territories. Yet they, more than most other critters might be expected to be territorial in their behaviors. Territoriality is far from universal in the animal kingdom. Rather than reaching far down the phylogenetic scale to embrace a concept that applies only irregularly and extend it unreservedly to basketball and soccer players seems a bit far fetched. On the other hand, if no other explanations were available, it might do in a pinch. However, the fact is that we do have several entirely reasonable explanations for the home field advantage.

The first explanation requires that we look closely at the actions of spectators vis a vis the local and visiting teams. Although promoters regularly urge a large turnout of fans to spur the local team to an inspired performance, the dynamics of what actually occurs appear to be something quite different. In sports where spectators typically cheer the locals and direct hostility and abuse at the visitors, we find that they have a greater impact on the performance of the visiting players. Larger and larger numbers in the stands do little to improve the play of the home team but do successfully impair the quality of the visitors' play. The influence of home town crowds then goes a considerable way toward accounting for the edge enjoyed by teams playing at home.

Another explanation is apparent to those who specialize in the study of human memory. It is called **context-dependent memory**. Quite simply, it means that we perform a behavior best in the situation in which the behavior was originally learned, less well in other situations. Considering that teams in most leagues practice and play half of their games in their own stadium, that is exactly where they should perform best.

The basic idea is seen in an ingenious study conducted by two Scottish psychologists. They had divers learn lists of words on land and underwater at a depth of 20 ft. Context-dependent memory would be evident if those learning the lists on land recalled better on land than underwater. Conversely, those learning underwater would be predicted to have better recalls underwater than on land. This is exactly what was found. Backed up by other research in this tradition, context-dependent memory provides us with a second, entirely plausible explanation for the home field advantage.

Yet another explanation involves several factors associated with travel. Anyone who has suffered from jet lag or taken a 10-hour bus ride knows all about the debilitating and demoralizing effects of travel. Players on the road sleep in unfamiliar surroundings, experience changes in diet and are separated from friends and family. All have the potential to impair an athlete's performance.

Personal experience tells us that jet lag likely has an impact on athletic performance, especially when athletes fly from West to East. This assumption was confirmed in the records of the National Football League. Game records from 1978 to 1987 were analyzed to determine the effects of time zone changes on the outcome of contests. As predicted, teams from the West were shown to play less well when they travelled to meet their Central and Eastern division opponents.

To round out the list of explanations for the home field advantage, I would direct your attention ahead to Chapter 26 entitled: "Judges: Favoring Their Own" (dealing with the decision-making of officials as it does, the topic seemed better suited to that section). Rather than repeat myself, I will simply affirm that officials can sometimes unwittingly, sometimes deliberately, contribute to the home field advantage.

To recap, the home field advantage is well established as an important factor affecting the outcome of contests in a number of sports. The leading explanations include the impact of fans' hostility toward visitors, context-dependent memory, officiating and several factors associated with travel. Depending on the circumstances and sport, any one, or combination of these explanations can account for the edge enjoyed by athletes competing at home.

9 The Championship Choke

There are times when the home field advantage is no advantage at all. In fact, in certain circumstances playing at home can be a major disadvantage. We can all remember an occasion when a home team, even with the enthusiastic support of its fans, somehow managed to snatch defeat from the jaws of victory in the final game. They choked, they folded, they booted it. Maybe next year will bring a reversal of fortunes.

But, the circumstances in which the home field advantage becomes the home field disadvantage are quite specific. It occurs for home teams on the brink of victory playing in the final game of a championship series. If they win, they are the champions of whatever for 2001. If they lose, they are unfortunately labelled as "losers" and quickly forgotten. It is this fear of failure, a fear that is strongest for teams playing in the presence of their loyal supporters, that can bring about their downfall. During the last game of a do or die championship series, players are acutely aware, especially if they fall behind in the score, that they are in imminent danger of acquiring a new identity, that of a loser. Errors creep into their play and their worst fear frequently becomes a reality.

Alternatively, it has been suggested that playing under the watchful eyes of enthusiastic and expectant supporters can cause an athlete to begin focussing on particular components of his performance. The local favorite, leading the field as his foursome begins the last nine holes of a regional golf tournament, starts to analyze his backswing, a swing that has already taken him to the top of the leader board. The results of this self-examination can, of course, be disastrous.

Finally, it may also be the case that boisterous fans anticipating their team's success may divert the athletes' attention away from the cues that are essential to an outstanding performance. For example, if our local golfer starts to visualize his name in tomorrow's headlines as he tees up on the dreaded 17th water hole, his name is quite likely to be in fine print.

The championship choke has been found to occur in both team and individual sports. Baseball teams in World Series competition and championship series in basketball show clear evidence of the home field disadvantage. Likewise, the play of British golfers in the British Open Golf Championship was found to deteriorate more than that of "foreign" players from the first through to the final round of the tournament.

10 When Praise Hurts

We all appreciate a little praise from time to time. Whether we are complimented for our appearance, our garden, a dinner we prepared or an assignment at the office, it is always satisfying to receive recognition for a job well done. Certainly, reinforcement theory sees occasional praise as an aid to learning a new skill. However, some evidence cautions against making sweeping generalizations regarding the use of praise in improving performance. It seems that while praise improves performance on certain tasks, on others it can instead prove harmful.

Recall if you will, the previous chapter in which the enthusiastic support of home town fans expecting victory was shown to bring about the downfall of their team in the final game of a championship series. It seems that praise also creates external pressure on athletes much as do home town fans, pressure that can disrupt a performance. But, whether praise helps or hurts a performance depends on the type of task.

The performance of tasks requiring a high level of skill have been shown to be hurt by praise. At the same time, the performance of tasks that depend mainly on effort is instead, improved by praise. Thus for example, it might be wise to withhold praise from a pole vaulter for succeeding at greater and greater heights. That same praise might be better saved for members of a tug-o-war team whose success in competition depends on an explosion of effort.

Similar to the dynamics underlying the championship choke, praise heightens the athlete's state of self-consciousness. As a consequence, our pole vaulter begins to pay attention to elements of his/her performance that were previously automatic. The result can be a disruption of a finely-tuned, coordinated performance. The researchers investigating this question leave us with a concluding thought that sums up what we should remember about praise: "Although praise is subjectively pleasant to receive, it appears to be a mixed blessing in terms of its effects on subsequent performance" (Baumeister, Hutton & Cairns, 1990, p. 147).

11   When 2 + 2 = 3

Team sports are a dominant feature of the contemporary sports scene. Individual talents are brought together and coordinated to produce an overall group result. Each team hopes that their combined efforts will produce a better result than that realized by their rivals in competition. The importance of each team member's contribution to the outcome is best seen in interdependent sports, e.g., relay events, where a poor performance by one athlete can put the entire team out of the running. For example, the award-winning fullback will no longer win awards if those blocking for him cease to give their best efforts. Success requires that each member of a team make a maximum effort. The combination of these individual efforts should in turn, produce a maximum result. But, does it?

In this case, the arithmetic that we all learned in primary school just doesn't add up. Let me describe one of the earliest studies in psychology that illustrates this very point. Imagine, if you will, only one of the teams competing in a tug-o-war. The "other team" is replaced by a fixed spring scale to be used for measuring the combined pull exerted by all team members. Before measuring a team effort, each member is first individually tested being asked to make their maximum pull against the spring scale. In the next stage, 2, 3 and 8- member teams are formed and again exhorted to make a maximum, collective effort. The results were not what we should expect.

Two-man teams exerted a combined force equal to only 93% of the total force of their individual maximum pulls. When a third member was added to the team, the total team force dropped to 85% while an 8-member team exerted only 49%

of the force one would expect by adding up what each man had demonstrated they were capable of pulling. The name given to this shortfall of effort is **social loafing**.

This strong tendency for team members to slacken off when performing in team competitions has been demonstrated in relay events in swimming and in track. Swimmers from a Big Ten university posted slower times when they competed as members of a relay team than when they swam in the individual events. Women sprinters also ran the 4 x 100m relay slower than would be expected on the basis of their individual 100m times. Interestingly, loafing still occurred even though complete details of the phenomenon were shared with the runners in advance of their event.

At this point, let's bring a squad of high school cheerleaders front and center to illustrate social loafing. This particular example involved girls who were attending a summer camp for cheerleaders. The study called for them to shout as loud as they could both alone and again, with other girls. In order to isolate the noise made by each girl in the team effort, they were misled into believing that they were shouting alongside other members of their squad. To achieve this they were blindfolded and wore soundproof headsets under the pretext of isolating them from any influence from the other members of their team. Was there evidence of social loafing? Once again, the girls held back when they believed they were shouting with others. When they were alone however, they gave it their all.

While we are on the topic of cheer leaders, have you ever wondered just how much noise a high school cheerleader can make? The authors of the study tell us that on the standard scale of loudness, the girls peaked at 102 decibels. To put this in perspective, that is equal to the roar of a New York subway train passing through a station.

While it appears that explaining to team members how social loafing works does not solve the problem for a coach, another possibility exists. One of the features of many interdependent team sports is that it is usually difficult to determine just how well each individual team member has performed on any single occasion. Unlike golf or ski teams where we know each member's score or time, in other sports such as football or rowing, it becomes extremely difficult to isolate and identify the caliber of individual performances. One's personal contribution is submerged and lost in the overall team effort. No one knows for sure how great an effort was made by each member of the team. Therein lies at least the possibility of a solution. If the coaching staff can somehow evaluate individual performances on a team and make such information available to teammates and others, then loafing is likely to disappear. Posting the individual times in relay events or isolating the game performance of a football linesman on camera for later analysis may prove effective. The trick is to be able to identify athletes with a measure of their performance and to make such information generally available. In sports such as rowing and tug-o-war, such advice is easier given than followed.

12 Who Really Won the Summer Olympics?

Nationalistic themes invariably creep into coverage of the Olympic Games. Seemingly determined to lead us away from the Olympic ideal, the international media provides its audiences with daily, often hourly, reports of the medal standings of the competing nations. Sometimes the standings are determined by the total number of medals won by each country; at other times the importance of each medal is weighted, i.e., gold (3), silver (2) and bronze (1).

Everyone recognizes that by the standard of medal counts past Olympics have generally been "won" by the rich and powerful nations, i.e., the Soviet Union, East Germany and the United States. However, medal counts virtually guarantee that smaller, poorer nations are left out in the cold. No account is taken of what they have been able to achieve despite small populations and few resources. Yet, each Olympic Games see one or two nations do amazingly well relative to their size and impoverished economies.

It was with a view to giving credit to countries that have *achieved much with little* that two Dutch economists proposed an alternative measure of a nation's Olympic achievement, one that takes into account a nation's well-being. The measure of a country's economic and social health incorporates factors such as income level, literacy rates and the life expectancy of its citizens, all adjusted for the size of its population. The measure was applied to the medal performances of those countries that competed in the 1988 (Seoul, South Korea) and 1992 (Barcelona, Spain) games. Some new names appear at the top of the final standings.

The winner of both Olympic games was *Kenya*. Second and third place at the Barcelona games went to Hungary and Cuba, respectively. By way of comparison, the final standings saw the former Soviet Union ranked 23rd respectively, while the United States placed 26th.

If we insist on pitting countries against each other then this system at least provides a more even playing field. For myself, I am more impressed with the Olympic achievements of those third world countries who despite almost insurmountable obstacles somehow manage to win medals.

Summary

In this section, I adopted a broader focus in dealing with more general factors that can affect overall team performance. We saw that the situation, e.g., home vs. away, fans expectations, and excessive praise can influence the level of athletic performance. The same can be said of a structural factor, e.g., team size, which in some sports can lead to a shortfall of effort. A concluding chapter presented a totally new and refreshing way of evaluating the performance of national teams in Olympic competition.

III. Secret Ingredients of Success

Introduction

Truly outstanding ability in a sport springs from an ideal combination of genetically inherited factors and the presence of conditions during the formative years that foster the development of whatever native talents the aspiring athlete might have. Some factors such as height, sex or reaction time are largely givens and to a great extent dictate which sport(s) offer the best opportunities for success. The 5 ft. 4 inch, "vertically-challenged" male has virtually no hope of playing alongside Michael Jordan. On the other hand, social and environmental factors, e.g., opportunities, coaching etc., can similarly determine the high point of an individual's athletic achievement. Despite an intense interest, those lacking considerable financial means will also find yachting, polo and show-jumping to be pretty much out of the question.

That ideal combination of genetic and social influences, of course, varies considerably from sport to sport. Nevertheless, sport researchers have devoted a large amount of their energies to the task of identifying one or more crucial ingredients that set the top flight athletes in a sport apart from those that fall just short of the mark. Each of the chapters to follow will highlight studies that have revealed critical differences between those who are outstanding in their sport and those who are ever so slightly less than outstanding. That is, what is that little something extra, that little bit of magic that one or two people in a sport have that sets them apart from the rest of the field?

13 Timing Is Everything

A number of sports place a premium on the ability to pace oneself. In the jargon of horse racing, it refers to a jockey's ability to "rate" horses. Once horses are up to speed after leaving the starting gate, there is a steady decline in speed all the way to the wire. The jockey who allows his horse too much early speed is apt to find his mount dying in the homestretch. The jockey who holds his horse back for too long may similarly find his horse finishing with extra speed left over. The trick then, is to get to the finish line with your mount being neither overextended nor finishing with speed to burn.

The ability to judge time intervals has been the subject of research for a great number of years. While people differ in this ability, it is a matter of continuing debate whether it is a learned or built-in skill. One school of thought suggests that each of us has an "internal clock". However, our clocks are not necessarily keeping the same time, some of us running a little fast, others a little slow. Two occupations that provide equal opportunities to learn and improve time judgment skills are jockeys and exercise riders (most exercise riders are either ex-jockeys or jockey wanabees). If jockeys' internal clocks are found to keep more accurate time than those of exercise riders, then the suggestion would be that the ability to rate horses is a critical factor in separating winning jockeys from those who consistently finish out of the money.

Jockeys and exercise riders agreed to participate in an exploratory, time estimation study. Both groups were of the same age and had the same years of riding experience. The main finding was that jockeys were better than exercise riders at judging time. There was also a hint that among the jockeys those with the most accurate internal clocks also had higher earnings.

This is not to suggest that the ability to rate horses is the only skill required for success as a jockey. Tactics vis a vis the other riders in the field can also be central to success. However, the influence of jockeys is not equal at all distances. Their influence is greater at the longer distances and has been shown to be especially strong on dirt tracks.

Of course, it is not only jockeys who can benefit from a good sense of time. This special ability may also provide an edge in sports such as harness racing, kayaking, rowing events, wrestling and boxing. The fighter being battered on the ropes may wisely cover-up, save his energy and postpone a rally if he "knows" the bell is about to sound. Thus, when competitors are equal in strength, speed, skill, etc., being able to accurately judge time may in some sports be the difference between winning and losing.

14   Ice-bergs: Searching for the Best

The ice-berg profile originates with a fairly straightforward notion, namely, that mentally healthy athletes perform better than those with some degree of psychopathology. Of course, the same might be said of people pursuing excellence in any field of endeavor.

Assessments are typically conducted using the Profile of Mood States (POMS), a measure that assesses five *negative* mood states, i.e., fatigue, anger, tension, confusion and depression, in addition to two *positive* mood states labelled vigor and self-esteem. Scores (norms) based on a large sample of the general population are often shown as a horizontal dotted line and represent the ocean surface or "water line". Mainly, outstanding athletes score below the general population on the scales measuring negative mood states but peak sharply above the norm on the vigor scale. Voila! .. an ice-berg.

Consider an example of how the POMS has been used in practise. Daniel Wann and his colleagues at Murray State University in Kentucky predicted that basketball fans who strongly identify with their team would exhibit the ice-berg profile indicative of psychological well-being. A less healthy profile was predicted for fans who only weakly identify with their team. The Figure below (adapted from Wann et al., 1999) shows the outline of an ice-berg with highly identified fans scoring higher on vigor and self-esteem. Overall then, they were credited with better psychological health.

For a time, it appeared that the measure was sensitive to the subtle differences in personality that set elite athletes apart from those falling just short of elite status. Thus for example, athletes who were Olympics bound exhibited a more pronounced ice-berg profile than those failing to qualify for an Olympic berth. However, more recently it would appear that this mental health approach

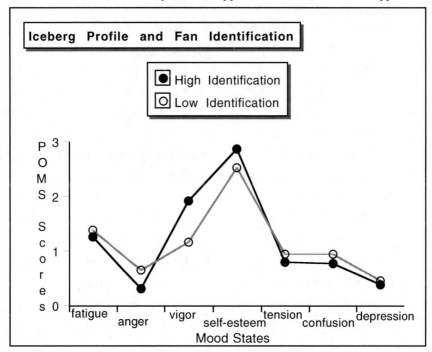

is only minimally able to predict performance in athletes. This conclusion was reached following an overall analysis of 33 ice-berg studies. When all the pluses and minuses (positive and negative results) from the studies were added up, the result only slightly favored the model. Still while applications of the model to the sports world should be undertaken with caution, the task of identifying that little something extra that characterizes the best of the best remains a formidable challenge. That challenge continues to be addressed with an updated and more promising dynamic mental health model.

15   Leaders Who (Don't) Fold Under Pressure

The conference football championship is on the line and time is running out in the fourth quarter. Your team is down by 5 points but has possession of the ball on their own 30 yard line with barely enough time left to move downfield for a winning touchdown. Unfortunately, your starting quarterback has just been helped to the dressing room with undetermined injuries. Sportscasters, players and fans are looking to you for your next move. You look to your bench. You are among the luckiest of coaches having been blessed with two talented and experienced, backup quarterbacks. As for football talent, they are equally gifted.

Bart is a sophomore majoring in economics who because of his love of football, decided to attend on an athletic scholarship (he had earlier turned down an offer of an academic scholarship). Throughout his college career Bart has maintained a straight A average. Teammate Dudley is also playing in his sophomore year on an athletic scholarship. His biggest worry has been remaining academically eligible for football. Putting the best light on it, his grades can best be described as mediocre. Under the pressure of the situation described above, who should get the call to go into the game, Bart or Dudley?

Pressure packed, do-or-die situations arise for most teams at some point in the season. From what you have been told about Bart and Dudley, the only thing separating them is intellectual ability. In all other respects they are equal. The question for you as a coach is which quarterback will perform best under the high stress conditions of the final minute. Do you want an exceptionally bright quarterback leading your team or one of average intelligence?

Some recent developments in leadership theory have looked specifically at the relationship between the leader's IQ and his/her performance under stress. Numerous studies including one in basketball, have produced some unexpected findings. It seems that in the vast majority of cases where leaders carry out their role in relatively nonstressful circumstances high intelligence, not surprisingly, is an asset. Their groups perform better than those led by low IQ leaders. However, under conditions of extreme stress, it is the low IQ leaders who get superior performances from their group. Yes, quarterback Dudley should get the call.

It seems that leaders of average intelligence are better able to draw from their experience in high stress situations. Guided by past experiences, they lead their followers to superior performances through periods of crisis. By contrast, high IQ leaders appear less able to draw from their previous experience and in a sense flounder under stress. One noted authority describes high IQ leaders as tending to "babble" when the pressures are extreme. Thus, while a high degree of intelligence makes for more effective leadership in most situations, crunch-time isn't one of them.

16 Brainpower at the Racetrack

Who makes the big money at the track? Most of us recognize the importance of knowledge and experience at the racetrack. Still, there is no shortage of losers among punters who study racing and have been gambling for years. Perhaps, those who come away "winners" are just plain smarter than the rest of us. That is, they are better able to figure out what is important in predicting the winner of a race and as a consequence make wagering decisions that more often result in a payoff. Just how important is I.Q.?

It would appear that one's I.Q. has little to do with picking winners. Smart people are not necessarily overrepresented among those who line up at the payout windows. Picking winners has much more to do with another intellectual skill. Simply put, some people deal with information in a complex way, others deal with the same information in a simple way. The point to keep in mind is that the complexity with which we process information is only weakly related to I.Q. This means then, that many highly intelligent people deal with information in a simple manner while many less intelligent people deal with information in a complex fashion.

Very briefly, the complex individual is one who can see things from another person's point of view and who is flexible in his/her thought processes. For example, they are able to change their minds on an issue in the light of new information rather than rigidly "sticking to their guns". They also tend to avoid what might be called "black - white" thinking. For example, the positions of others on an issue are not lumped into the two categories of those for 'em and those agin 'em but rather shades of differences or gradations of opinion are recognized and taken into account. Thus, they realize that the truth of a matter often lies somewhere in between two extreme, either/or categories. Last but not least, the complex person seems better able to hold off on a decision allowing more information to be taken into consideration.

The authors of this investigation note that four of their expert handicappers had IQs in the low to mid 80s. For example, "... a construction worker with an IQ of 85 who had been a regular at the track for 16 years, picked the top horse in terms of post-time odds in 10 out of 10 races and picked the top three horses in correct order 5 out of 10 races". By contrast, an nonexpert "... lawyer with an IQ of 118 who had been going to the track regularly for 15 years, correctly picked the top horse in only 3 out of 10 races and the top three horses in only 1 out of 10 races" (Ceci & Liker, 1986, p. 262). While those blessed with a high level of intelligence excel at many endeavors, they do no better than the rest of us when it comes to playing the ponies.

17 Optimism Wins

Few people would dispute the common belief that psychological factors often play a decisive role in affecting athletic performance. The mental part of a sport is every bit as important to success as the physical component. Whether or not one holds an optimistic view of events -- be they good (wins) or bad (losses) -- is one such mental factor.

Athletes and people generally have over the years acquired their own particular explanatory style by which they offer typically optimistic or pessimistic explanations for events. Consider the explanation offered by a pessimistic athlete for a bad event, i.e., a loss. First, "it was my fault" (internal), second, "we are going to continue losing" (stable) and third, "what caused the loss is going to affect everything that happens to me" (global). On the other hand, the optimistic athlete is going to explain the loss in the opposite way. He sees the bad event as caused by someone else (external), sees it as short-lived (unstable) and believes the cause is only going to influence this particular event (specific).

How do athletes' optimistic or pessimistic explanatory styles affect them in the win/loss column? Starting with basketball, National Basketball Association teams who collectively held a more optimistic view of bad events, i.e., losses, were found to perform better in their next game following a loss than did teams with a pessimistic view. An optimistic explanatory style was also related to the performance of major league baseball teams. Those teams with an optimistic explanatory style for good and bad events in one season went on to win more games than pessimistic teams during the next season of play.

The sport of swimming provided a further opportunity to see whether a sense of optimism affects individual athletes in the same way as it affects teams. Clearly, it does. Over a season of competition, the performance of swimmers with a pessimistic style fell below what was anticipated by their coaches. Optimistic swimmers were closer to their coach's expectations. Also, following "rigged" time trials that led swimmers to believe they had a slow time (a bad event), the performance of those with a pessimistic outlook worsened whereas optimists maintained their earlier levels.

Several additional points regarding optimism are worth noting. Although optimism is generally seen as a trait acquired through life experiences, it may also be a part of our genetic inheritance. Furthermore, whether we are optimistic or pessimistic can greatly influence the state of our health. Optimists are generally less likely to be afflicted with such illnesses as anxiety, depression, coronary heart disease and yes, even the common cold. This favorable influence on health leads us to the further question of whether optimists perhaps live longer than pessimists? There is good evidence that they in fact, do. Comments made in interviews to the press by members of the St. Louis Baseball Hall of Fame for the period 1900-1950 were assessed for optimistic content. Those players expressing optimism in response to positive events during their playing days easily outlived their less optimistic teammates (see also, Chapter 61 for more on longevity).

18   The Winning Edge in Golf

What part of your golf game is the key to a low handicap? Is it important to be long off the tee? Perhaps it's not length that counts but rather keeping the ball on the fairway? Maybe executing shots from the sand traps is the key to success. Hitting the greens in regulation or putting may also be the mark of a championship golfer. Indeed, the old adage "drive for show, putt for dough" suggests that experience points to putting as the skill that sets tournament winners apart from the rest of the field. Which of the sub-skills that are brought into play during a round of golf best predict a player's total score or, for that matter, tournament earnings?

Measures of all the golfing sub-skills noted above were derived from the PGA Tour Official Statistics Profile for a 3 year period. The single skill most strongly associated with a low scoring average was hitting greens in regulation. While the remaining skills were also associated with low averages, they were clearly less important. Hitting greens in regulation was followed, in order, by driving accuracy, number of putts per round, sand save percentages and average distance of drives.

The picture is somewhat muddied by two more recent studies comparing the top ten professionals to the bottom ten on both the North American and European PGA tours. The top money winners on the North American tour were superior to those at the bottom on two skills, driving distance and a measure of total driving. The top ten money winners on the PGA European tour were also superior to those at the bottom of the money list in driving distance and total driving. However, they also hit more greens in regulation and made more sand saves.

Would the same pattern of skills that separate winning pros from others in the tournament field also apply to weekend golfers? At this point we can't say with certainty. Meanwhile, speaking as someone who in years gone by struggled to break 80, I would go with the "greens in regulation" finding. In my humble opinion a little extra time in practice working on your long irons could easily knock a couple of strokes off your handicap.

Perhaps, we casual golfers stand to learn more from a study that questioned men whose average handicap was 16 (range 5 to 27). Five important differences were found between the high and low handicap golfers. Those more skilled golfers (lower handicaps) show a stronger *commitment* to the sport in, e.g., expressing a preference for competitive over social golf. Furthermore, they exhibit better *mental preparation*, e.g., a consistent preshot routine, and greater *concentration*, e.g., not easily distracted. The better golfers are also burdened less by *negative emotions*. For them, stepping up on the first tee is not the nerve wracking experience it is for most duffers. However, the single, most outstanding feature of skilled players is *automaticity*. Their swing is well-grooved, automatic and they share a belief they could almost drive blindfolded.

Summary

As should be apparent from the foregoing chapters, "secret" ingredients is something of a misnomer. Rather, the secret ingredients are factors that simply are not generally recognized as sometimes being critical for a successful or optimum performance. They do not provide the means for an individual to suddenly unlock a reserve of previously unavailable talent. In the case of jockeys, quarterbacks and golfers, the special abilities mentioned above that may provide them with a competitive edge are either genetic in origin or developed over a considerable number of years within the context of the socialization process. As a consequence, efforts to instill these abilities or traits through training may require more time and effort than is reasonable with only a modest likelihood of success.

IV. Tips on Improving Performance

Introduction:

The sports section of bookstores are crammed with "how to win" books and books by commercially-minded superstars anxious to share the "secrets" of their success. It is not my intention to compete with this dubious array of performance enhancing works. Neither is this section an attempt to provide a comprehensive coverage of all that is known about improving athletic performance. My goal is far less ambitious; merely to pass along a small sample of well established tactics that some of you may wish to try on your own.

None of these tactics will transform you into an overnight sensation. However, you might add a point or two to your bowling average or shave a few seconds off your cross country time. What can be said about the suggestions is that they are based on the findings of competent researchers from a variety of fields. Whether or not they will work in the individual case will depend upon the sport certainly, as well as numerous other considerations. I leave it to you the reader to decide if a particular suggestion is useful in your case.

19 Golfers' Yips

The setting was the US Open Golf Championship in Rochester. Playing the 71st hole, Ben Hogan needed two pars to force a playoff with Dr. Cary Middlecoff. A par and a birdie would give him the title. A 30-inch putt remained for par and then, on to the final hole. Hogan lined up the short putt, then stood over the ball. By all accounts, his hands seemingly froze. He backed away. On a second try, his hand "jerked" on the putt and the Open was lost. Did the pressure get to him? Did he choke? Were his nerves shot?

The answer is none of the above. What was witnessed on that day was a classic case of the yips. Essentially, it is a neurological event that plagues perhaps as many as 30% of golfers as well as those engaged in a number of other occupations such as violinists, telegraphers and writers (writer's cramp).

Drawing generously from the writings of neurologist Dr. Harold Klawans (1996), the yips are a type of *dystonia* and represent "...a group of abnormal, involuntary movements with specific characteristics ... They are sudden pulls or jerks that move part of a limb into an untoward position and keep it there" (p. 100). It is primarily during putting in pressure-packed situations that some golfers experience the dreaded yips. The act of putting itself involves "... maintaining a relatively fixed posture, and at the same time superimposing on this posture, on the same muscles that are maintaining the posture, a delicately controlled movement" (pp. 103-104). It is this combination that brings out the abnormal movement.

Although the physiological bases of this neurological disorder are not well understood, golfers afflicted with the yips should nevertheless take heart. In keeping with the theme of this section, I can offer a few tips for those stricken with the yips. A variety of tactics that hold some promise of success have been suggested. These tactics have the effect of changing the input, in a sense they fool the brain. Included among the tricks are changing the grip on your putter, changing to a heavier putter, putting cross handed or perhaps, switching to a pendulum putter. One noted authority cautions against the use of hypnotherapy noting that he knows "...of no neurological problem for which hypnotherapy has ever been demonstrated to have any significant long-term efficacy. Why should yips be any different?" (Klawans, 1996, p. 107). The point is to actively experiment until you find something that works for you.

Whether you are a weekend duffer or a touring professional, you may find yourself spending as much time and energy struggling to overcome the yips as you are working on your golf game. Be assured that whether you are a Ben Hogan, a Sam Snead or a 24 handicapper, the problem is neurological in origin and does not represent a lack of nerves on your part. Better still, there is every reason to expect that your yips can be controlled.

20 Caffeine and Performance

Have you recorded disappointing times in recent middle or long distance events? Have your clockings in cross-country or cycling competitions been slower than what would be expected from your training? Let me offer a modest suggestion that may improve your times.

A surprising amount of research has been conducted on the effects of caffeine. However, not all of that research has shown that caffeine enhances all types of athletic performance. Where caffeine does appear to benefit the athlete is in endurance events. It also appears that caffeine is associated with a reduced perception of effort. Even ingesting a relatively small amount of caffeine can significantly affect one's endurance. Indeed, it appears that consuming increasingly larger doses adds nothing further to the performance level already achieved with a small dose.

It should be noted that caffeine is a restricted but not totally banned substance in the eyes of the International Olympic Committee and other regulatory bodies. In order to reach the doping limit of the IOC, the athlete would have to consume approximately 8 cups of coffee prior to testing. However, this number is well beyond the number of cups needed for improvement. Bearing in mind the unwelcome side effects of dizziness, headaches, tremors and gastric upset, 1-2 cups of coffee consumed prior to competition should be sufficient to have the desired effect. As regards additional cups providing further gains, more is not better.

21 "The Little Engine That Could"

> *And the Little Blue Engine smiled and seemed to say as she puffed*
> *steadily down the mountain ... "I thought I could. I thought I*
> *could. I thought I could. I thought I could. I thought I could. I*
> *thought I could. I thought I could"*

The Little Engine That Could (1976).

As personal performance factors go, **self-efficacy** is probably the single best ingredient, after ability, for predicting success in athletics. Work on the topic was pioneered by Stanford psychologist Albert Bandura whose formal definition of perceived self-efficacy follows:

"...people's judgments of their capabilities to organize and execute courses of action required to attain designated types of performances. It is concerned not with the skills one has but with judgments of what one can do with whatever skills one possesses" (Bandura, 1986, p. 391).

What is apparent from this definition is that self-efficacy is not the same as the commonly used term "self-confidence". To illustrate, of the two sports in which I participate, I may feel highly efficacious in golf, much less so in my attempts to master the skills of rock climbing. At the same time, I may be described across all situations as average on a trait of self-confidence. So one may feel highly efficacious in one situation (or, at one point in time), yet experience a low sense of efficacy in other circumstances (or, on other occasions). On the other hand, the trait of self-confidence is a relatively stable and enduring feature of the individual's personality.

From time to time we catch a glimpse of self-efficacy operating in the sportsworld. Examples of athletes who have lapsed into a slump that seems to go on forever can be found in virtually every sport. Other athletes never quite regain their previous form following an injury or "close call". Still other athletes baffle their coach and supporters with great performances in practice but only mediocre performances in actual competition. The common thread running through these examples is a low sense of self-efficacy. High self-efficacy is sometimes seen when a self-assured athlete with average ability upsets the highly skilled, but doubting, star favored to win the event. The athlete's self judgment regarding their capabilities then is frequently a critical factor in determining the outcome of competition.

Several other features make the development of self-efficacy an attractive goal. Those who have developed a strong sense of personal efficacy typically make a greater effort in taking up a new challenge. Furthermore, when their efforts meet with failure, they persist, showing an equal if not a greater effort on their next attempt. Those with low self-efficacy all but give up when their initial attempts are unsuccessful. In addition to showing persistence in attempting to master a skill, those with high self-efficacy are also better able to manage pain, sometimes a requirement in an athlete's job description.

For those not already familiar with Bandura's work, the practical question that springs to mind is how can one's sense of personal self-efficacy be increased for an activity. At the risk of oversimplification, a brief sketch of several tactics is provided for the benefit of interested coaches and athletes. The best method is to structure the situation so that the athlete's efforts in training meet with frequent success. In a very real sense, success breeds success. As we reach attainable goals we experience a strengthening of self-efficacy that can in turn, allow us to reach slightly higher goals. Thoughtful coaches can set a graduated series of goals for their charges, each small step being only incrementally more difficult than the previous one. With success nearly always following on the heels of a previous success, the athlete should experience an increase in self-efficacy for the activity. However, not every training trial need meet with success. Success that comes too easily does not equip us to weather the occasional setbacks and failures that inevitably mark progress in a sport.

In a sense, self-efficacy has to be carefully nurtured. For example, it would be extremely unwise to put an unseasoned rookie into a pressure-packed game in hopes of salvaging a victory. The possible short term gain is heavily outweighed by the consequences of failure for the rookie. Self-efficacy stands to be seriously undermined with the result that the rookie's early promise may never be realized.

Other tactics that have been shown to foster increased self-efficacy include the observation of others succeeding and, persuasion that one possesses the capabilities to perform successfully. Watching a model execute a performance that we ourselves are attempting to master can in some circumstances strengthen self-efficacy. Feelings of personal efficacy can also be strengthened when a coach convinces a doubting athlete that they possess the wherewithal to achieve a higher standard of performance. However, the tactic is fraught with dangers. Unrealistic appraisals open the door to possible failure and a consequent lowering of self-efficacy. The key is to provide appraisals that are in keeping with the athlete's current level of skill thus ensuring that success is much more likely than failure.

Finally, while others may have doubts about your state of mind, talking to yourself is not a bad idea. Positive self-talk along the lines of "I can do it", "I can finish", etc., can increase self-efficacy through a strengthened belief that one can perform the requisite behaviors. However, saying does not necessarily result in believing. The strengthened belief in one's capabilities must be consistent with the available evidence. That is, what you are attempting to do must be within reach, e.g., a personal best in the long jump, bowling a 200 game, etc. So, while dedication, hard work and native ability are important contributors to achievement, we should not lose sight of self-efficacy as an additional ingredient that can allow us to attain even higher goals than we perhaps aspired to.

22 Larks and Owls

Most of us would have little difficulty classifying ourselves as either morning persons (larks) or evening persons (owls). Larks find they do their best work early in the day; they think better and work more efficiently. Owls find they just can't get going in the morning but come to life in the late afternoon or early evening. What likely underlies these time preferences for tackling tasks are circadian rhythms.

What is meant by circadian rhythms are various physical and psychological cycles that occur over a 24-hour period. In addition to a sleep-wake cycle and blood cortisol levels, body temperature also follows a daily cycle reaching a peak and a low point at specific times. The body temperature cycle in particular is related to a number of factors such as oxygen consumption rate and grip strength that appear to affect athletic performance. Since body temperature peaks in the late afternoon or early evening for a majority of people, we might expect "personal bests" or record performances to more frequently be established late in the day. What evidence is there that such might be the case?

Consider first the results of an Irish study of an elite group of outstanding male and female swimmers preparing for their national championships. Twenty two swimmers competed in the four traditional events, i.e., backstroke, butterfly, breaststroke and free style. The racing trials called for a maximum effort and were conducted either in the morning and evening of the same day or, in the evening and the following morning. Across all days of the study, performances in the events were decidedly better at 17.00 hours. Faster times were recorded for 61 of the 85 clockings whereas 23 of the times were slower in the afternoon (1 swimmer swam identical times). Overall, there is much to recommend the late afternoon as the time for swimmers to attempt to better their times. However, the apparent advantage of late afternoon is not restricted to swimmers. Others have reported better performances by runners, shot putters and rowers. Maximum efforts in these sports were made by men and women in two time periods between 7.00 and 8.00 hours and, between 17.00 and 19.00 hours. All athletes turned in superior performances in the late afternoon/early evening.

Again, the most detailed assessment of athletic performance in relation to the time of day comes to us from the United Kingdom. And again, the sport of swimming has provided the setting for the research. This time the swimmers made an all-out effort in the front crawl at five different times during the day. Eight days of trials were conducted and spread over an entire month. The times at which the swims were staged were also randomized. We see in the Figure below

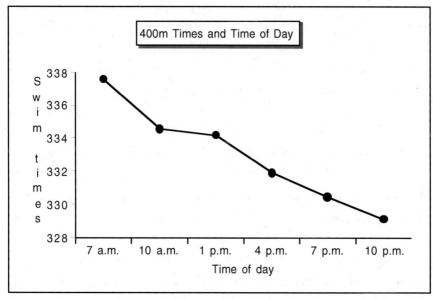

(adapted from Baxter & Reilly, 1983) that times in the 400m event steadily improved from early morning to late evening (7.00 to 22.00 hours). It is worth noting that faster times continued to be set very late into the evenings. As a consequence the authors recommend that "...where absolute performance levels are important, such as attempts to attain qualifying standards for major championships, is that these events should be fixed for evening rather than afternoon times" (Baxter & Reilly, 1983, pp. 125-126). I might emphasize, late evening.

23 Practice Makes Perfect

Coaches and athletes alike recognize the importance of practice in improving skills in a sport. However, they are generally less aware of how best to go about that task, i.e., how to organize components of their practice sessions so as to maximize the effectiveness of training. A wealth of research from the field of human learning provides a strong recommendation for those perfecting their athletic skills. The phenomenon itself is called **contextual interference**.

When several motor skills are being learned in the same practice session, a question arises as to whether each skill should be practiced separately as a group or, in a random order. For example, in batting practice is it better for the batter to be given 25 fast balls, then 25 curve balls, and lastly 25 change ups or, have all three types of pitches thrown in a random order?

What is typically found is a superior performance in practice by batters receiving grouped pitches, i.e., first the fast balls, next the curve balls and then the change ups. In this acquisition or practice stage, presenting the three types of pitches in sequence appears to be the best method. However, to everyone's surprise, when the results of practice sessions that used either the grouped or the random method are compared at a later date, the random method of practice is shown to have been clearly superior. Of course, batters facing pitchers in actual games have no knowledge of the next pitch. Batting success is to a large extent determined by the ability to first identify and then to react quickly to an incoming pitch. Thus, practice sessions in which batters attempt to hit different pitches delivered in a random fashion (much as occurs under game conditions) will lead to a better performance in competition.

Greater improvement in other sports can also be realized with different elements being practiced in a random order. Curlers might throw out turns, in turns, takeouts and draws in random order during practice as might tennis players hone their skills by randomly hitting backhands, forehands and lobs. So while practice is important to success, *how* you practice may be more important.

Summary

Each of the chapters in this section contained a tip(s) that potentially can improve an athlete's performance to some slight degree. Of course, they are not a substitute for training, practice and good coaching. Still, if you are trying to knock a stroke off your golf score or a second off your 800-meter time, something from the foregoing chapters may bring that about.

We turn now from matters of athletic performance to questions of its measurement. In the next section, the measuring device is not a stopwatch, a tape measure or a weigh scale but a human. Judges, referees, umpires, all are called upon to make decisions regarding the athlete's performance. We'll see how well they do.

V. The Decision Makers

Introduction:

Let me be clear at the outset. With rare exception, judges, referees and umpires are scrupulously honest in making their decisions. Whether serving an amateur or professional sport, they typically have extensive training and experience and make every effort to carry out their duties in a professional and impartial manner. Alas, they are also human!

In their role as interpreters of the "Rules of Play", they are essentially acting as measurement devices. While the electronic timing devices used in the 800-meter run or in the swimming pool are extremely precise, we recognize almost immediately that when human decision makers are used they necessarily fall somewhat short of that degree of perfection. The electronic timer cannot be influenced by partisan crowds and/or complaining athletes nor does it have knowledge of the athlete's reputation or press clippings. Humans however, are open to subtle influences from these sources, influences that can directly affect the judgments of sport officials.

Two further points deserve mention. Different sports make quite different demands on judges. In some sports officials are exposed to the hostile outbursts of irate fans and occasionally, athletes; in other sports, decisions are not openly challenged by spectators. Also, the complexity of the judges' tasks vary considerably from sport to sport. For example, the fast-paced action of basketball and ice hockey likely taxes the limits of a referee's ability to simultaneously follow the actions of ten or more players with an eye to rule violations. Other slower-paced sports such as golf and weight lifting are conducted in a less complex environment and allow sufficient time for judges to make unhurried and carefully considered decisions.

The chapters to follow then, highlight the impact that social influences and the judges' own expectations can have on the accuracy of decision making. But, let me emphasize that these influences operate for the most part without officials recognizing or even being aware of their existence. These potentially biasing influences have only been revealed by the carefully conducted research of social scientists. Our first example comes from gymnastics.

24 Pygmalion on the Balance Beam

We all have expectations regarding the likelihood of successful or unsuccessful performances by ourselves and by others. Typically, our expectations are formed on the basis of what we know about peoples' past behaviors. These expectations can in turn, set in motion a subtle pattern of social interactions that bring about the very result that was anticipated. This self-fulfilling nature of our expectations for the behavior of others is much stronger than is commonly recognized.

To illustrate. Expectations can be seen at work in a summer camp for boys and girls, ages 7-14. One of the activities at the camp was a swimming program in which the youngsters could earn a Red Cross Beginners swimming certificate. For purposes of creating expectations, the swimming instructors were given bogus test information indicating that half of the youngsters showed a superior potential for becoming good swimmers; for the remaining youngsters, no such information was provided to their instructors. By the end of the 2-week program, those who were expected to do well, had indeed, developed into decidedly better swimmers. Bear in mind that the two groups were randomly formed and additionally, that the instructors did not consciously treat the two groups any differently. Also note that the children's progress at the end of the program was independently assessed by external means. Their individual ability levels were determined by the 21 graduated subtests of specific skills they must pass in order to receive a Red Cross beginning swimmer's card.

Like anyone else, judges too have expectations. The question for sports events that are judged is whether judges' expectations can influence their ratings of athletic performance. To illustrate that possibility, consider the case of gymnastics. Over the years the traditional practice in team competition has been for coaches to order the appearance of their gymnasts from the weakest to the strongest team member. This practice has understandably led judges to "expect" to see the weaker gymnasts first and the better gymnasts, last on a teams program. However, when performances are recorded on videotape, it is an easy matter to reverse the order of a team's appearance. This was, in fact, done.

Nationally certified judges were asked to rate a series of gymnastic performances. For half of the teams, the order of appearance was reversed. The results were surprising. The judges' expectations formed an important part of their judgments. Those gymnasts who performed their routines last in their team's order received substantially higher marks than when they performed the identical videotaped routines first in the order. Thus, even with the best of intentions and a wealth of experience, judges are vulnerable to influence in their decisions. In this case a source of bias is seen to originate with their own expectations. Despite their best efforts to be completely objective and impartial, expectations can seemingly creep into their decisions and bias the results of competition.

25 Judges: A Patriotic Bias?

Overheard in from of an American TV set:

"Look at that! The Russian judge gave our Debbie only a 5.5"

Overheard in front of a Russian TV set:

Смотри! Американскии суд'я подал нашеи Ол'ге тол'ко 5.5

Millions of viewers world wide sit glued to the television screen during the Olympic Games and world championships in a variety of sports. International competition played at this elite level frequently stirs patriotic feelings such that we find ourselves pulling for athletes from our own country. International judges too are often suspected of pulling just a little too hard for athletes from their own country. This, despite their extensive experience and training that requires them to be completely objective and impartial in evaluating athletic performances. Mutterings of discontent with the panel of international judges frequently reverberate through sports such as figure skating, diving, synchronized swimming and gymnastics. Do these suspicions have some basis in fact or are they just sour grapes from disgruntled patriots?

It turns out that our suspicions are well founded, at least in figure skating and gymnastics. What appears to some to be a nationalistic bias whereby judges favor their fellow countrymen indeed occurs at the highest levels of international competition. This conclusion was reached in a study that examined the figure skating records of the 1984 (Sarajevo) and 1988 (Calgary) Winter Olympics. The bias was evident in both the men's and women's results in all segments of the competitions, i.e., compulsory figures, short program and the free skate portion of their programs.

The ways in which a nationalistic bias was determined are interesting. For example, if judges are totally impartial, then judges scoring skaters from their own country should be above the average scores of the remaining judges 50% of the time and below the average 50% of the time. This didn't happen. Rather, judges were found to award marks to skaters from their homeland that were well above the average marks awarded by the remaining panel members.

Another way of detecting bias was to look at the number of times that judges gave skaters representing their country the highest score from among all 9 judges on the panel. If they were completely impartial, then on a purely chance basis they would award the highest score to their countrymen only 1/9th (or 11%) of the time. Again, that didn't happen. Instead, when skaters and judges came from the same country, judges favored their athletes with maximum scores well beyond what would be expected from impartial judges.

But, were all countries guilty of showing favoritism toward their nationals? The answer is "yes" although some were found to be less guilty than others. Those showing the least amount of bias were those that had the fewest skaters entered in the Olympic competition (e.g., Belgium, France, Italy and Sweden). By contrast, judges from nations that had three or more skaters showed a stronger bias favoring their own skaters (e.g., Canada, the Federal Republic of Germany, the German Democratic Republic, Japan, the USSR and the USA).

The problem of international bias is not however, confined to skating. Gymnastics has seen it share of biased officiating. The records of the 1984 Olympic gymnastics competition also revealed a clear international bias. Judges, both male and female, awarded scores to their own athletes that "...were higher than the average scores of the remaining members of their panels 282 times and lower on 29 times" (Ansorge & Scheer, 1988, p. 105).

Is there a solution to the problem? Yes there is one that, while it is not perfect, would go a long way toward removing national bias. One reasonable solution lies with using a trimmed average. Trimming simply involves dropping the highest and the lowest score for each competitor, much as is the current practice in synchronized swimming. Officials in skating, gymnastics and other events involving international panels of judges would do well to give serious consideration to improving their scoring procedures. Otherwise, we cannot be assured that only the best performers on the day step up on the victory rostrum.

26 Judges: Favoring Their Own

Basketball referees and officials in other sports are not immune to the pressure of home town fans anxious for a victory. Furthermore, in the case of basketball, referees themselves are an important factor contributing to the well known, home court advantage (other contributing factors were discussed in detail in Chapter 8). An examination of National Basketball Association records shows a strong bias by referees, one that favors the home team.

Fans and officials alike are aware of the fact that it is the "star" players on a team who are in the best position to produce a victory. When the number of fouls awarded players are compared between home and away games, a clear pattern of biased officiating is seen. While nonstar players are penalized equally often at home and away, the star players draw fewer fouls on their home court. Obviously, there is a considerable advantage for the home team when their stars remain on the court late in a game while the visiting stars are benched.

Some of my readers will be quick to raise the possibility that visiting stars are given more playing time than they are given back in their home arenas. If that is the case then certainly, more penalties would be expected with longer playing time. However, the authors did their homework. The official records indicate that the star players overall had equal playing time at home and away games.

Further evidence of biased officiating is seen in a study of 950 international cricket matches played from 1877 to 1980. In several countries visiting batsmen were more likely to be called out than those batting for the home team. However, the study leaves open the possibility that different playing conditions and styles may have accounted for the umpires' decisions. As an aside, the researchers offer anecdotal evidence of umpires being pressured by sport officials to deliberately favor the home team in their judgments. On one occasion, "Pakistani umpires resigned alleging that they had been coerced by their Cricket Board to 'see' things the way of their own team" (Sumner & Mobley, 1981, p. 29).

It seems that biased officiating is not confined to a particular sport or culture. In the case of Australian rules football we again see evidence that game officials can show bias in favor of members of their own group, in this instance teams from their own state. We know from previous studies that social judgments are affected by one's group membership such that people tend to favor, perceive, and evaluate members of their own group more favorably than outgroup members.

Umpires consistently gave preferential treatment over several seasons of play to teams from their own region. An interesting pattern of favoritism was seen when a zone by zone comparison of free kicks was made. The local teams were awarded an excess of free kicks in their defensive rather than their attacking zones. Thus, the threat of scoring by out-of-state teams was in many cases thwarted. The researchers suggest that umpires were aware that a biased decision awarded the ingroup in their attacking zone would be more easily recognized as such and instead, chose to favor the ingroup in a less obvious way. Thus, we see in these findings several examples of how game officials can unwittingly, and sometimes deliberately, introduce an element of bias into their decisions.

27 When to Pull the Goalie

The clock is ticking down and the midget hockey team you agreed to coach this season is one goal down to their long-time rivals. What to do? Hockey wisdom has it that you should pull your goalie in favor of getting an extra attacker in the last minute of play. If you can salvage a tie, then at least you get one point in the league standings or force an overtime. Otherwise, if your opponent scores while your goalie is sitting on the bench, the result of a two goal loss is no different than losing by one goal, i.e., zero points in the standings.

The fans, your players, everyone in the arena is looking to you for a decision. Of course, the safest tactic is to stick with tradition and pull your goalie in the last minute of play. Then again, you may want to opt for what appears to be a much riskier tactic and bench the goalie much earlier, say with 2 minutes of playing time remaining. Hockey buffs with high-level mathematical credentials tell us that you are on the right track although, in fact, you haven't gone far enough. The most recent calculations indicate that the best point at which to pull the goalie in hopes of gaining a tie is 2:34 minutes before the final whistle. Even if you are two goals behind, don't despair. The tactic can still be successful. In this case, the recommendation is to bench your goalie with 2:30 to 3 minutes remaining.

Of course, there are no guarantees. In fact, the actual gain to be had by following the results of these calculations is only a 10% improvement over waiting until the last minute. Still, championships are frequently won and lost by the proverbial whisker. Incidentally, if you try this and it backfires, please don't call me. I am only the messenger.

28 And the Winner by a Split Decision is____

Typically following a close boxing match, the loser's manager seizes the interviewer's mike to claim: "We was robbed. My boy was ahead all the way. We want a rematch". Is this anything more than a standard ploy to make the fight appear closer than it perhaps, was? If doubts can be raised about the fairness of the judges' decision, then a rematch becomes a distinct possibility. The rematch of course, usually means another hefty paycheck for those in the boxer's camp.

Similar charges have been levelled at ring officials in international competitions. Certainly, most of us are convinced that a strong nationalistic bias has crept into the decisions of Olympic judges at the boxing as well as at other sports venues. We have seen over the years with distressing regularity, controversy, charges and counter charges of national favoritism on the part of those judging athletic contests. But, is there more going on here than a nationalistic bias. Is there something to the manager's claim that the judges are near-sighted or worse, blind? In fact, there is good reason to believe that yet another factor is contributing to the controversial decisions that for years have plagued boxing.

The key question I am raising is whether those judging a match are pretty much in agreement in their scoring of the fight. They are, after all, watching the same bout, albeit from somewhat different angles. Let's follow the steps taken by researchers in their efforts to determine just how consistent boxing judges are in their task of evaluating boxing skill by means of the established system of awarding points.

The particular fight chosen represented the sport at the highest level. In 1971 heavyweight champion Muhammed Ali faced challenger Joe Frazier in Manila, Philippines in what became known as the "Thrilla in Manila". The stakes were high. Enormous prestige and literally millions of dollars hung on the outcome. Ali lost his title by an unanimous decision following the 15 round bout.

With so much riding on the fight, it is not unreasonable to expect that the measures of boxing skill -- the referee and two judges at ringside -- would be in fairly high agreement on each fighter's round by round score over the course of the fight. How did they do? In a word, terrible! The results did not even approach anything resembling an acceptable level of inter-judge agreement. It simply means that the decision could just as easily have gone to Ali; the measure provided by ring officials was just that shaky.

However, there are steps that could be taken to improve this situation. For example, simply increasing the number of judges at ringside would raise the reliability of ratings overall. Also, having the judges score both halves of each round separately could improve their level of agreement. While these suggestions have been around since at least 1972, the boxing world has thus far shown no interest. Meanwhile, controversial decisions continue to be the rule.

29 Pitchers' Reputations and the Strike Zone

There are times in the life of a baseball umpire that are decidedly unpleasant. Standing behind home plate, a close call - either way - can result in stormy debate and personal abuse from players, coaches and fans. Still, umpires must remain firm in their decisions. To give in to the pressure and change their mind is only to invite more conflict in the future. They must at least appear to be supremely confident of their calls and unmovable in the face of disagreement. But try as they might, umpires like the rest of us, are social animals open to influences from others (recall the expectancy effects of Chapter 24 above). One such social influence is the reputation that the pitcher brings to the mound.

Over time, umpires get to know a great deal about pitchers in the league from personal experience behind the plate. Of course, umpires also read the sports pages. Certain pitchers become known for their erratic performance on the mound. Certainly, they throw strikes but other pitches are far outside the strike zone. They soon establish a reputation for wildness. By contrast, other pitchers are known for their control, their pitches being either called in or barely missing the strike zone. Would a pitcher's reputation for wildness or control in any way influence the umpire behind the plate? On close calls, would he tend to call the same pitch a ball for the wild pitcher and a strike in the case of the control pitcher? Such is the common belief of coaches and players and, the prediction made by a John Carroll University research team.

Pitchers' reputations were established by having certified umpires watch a series of videotaped "warm-up" pitches, one demonstrating wildness, the other demonstrating a controlled performance. With reputations set firmly in the minds of the umpires, they then proceeded to call a series of 68 pitches. The results caught everyone by surprise. Just the opposite to what was predicted actually occurred. Close pitches by pitchers known to be wild were called as strikes; close pitches by controlled pitchers were called as balls.

Why umpires apparently open up the strike zone for a wild pitcher and shrink it for a control pitcher is open to speculation. Before answers are sought for this counter-intuitive finding however, we might first hope to see it repeated in another part of the country and with umpires working with youngsters and/or professional teams. Although the result is preliminary, I like this study for again showing that human behavior in sports is not always what it seems. As shown here and elsewhere in this book, there are surprises around most corners.

30 Out at First... Well, Not Necessarily

The short stop momentarily juggles the ball before the throw to first base. Although the call is close, the runner is OUT! The call is hotly disputed by the manager though tempers eventually cool and the game continues. However, those of us in the television audience are given the opportunity to call the play ourselves through the miracle of slow motion replays. What we sometimes find is that regardless of the camera angle, the runner was clearly safe. To be sure, the umpire did not have the benefit of the latest in media technology.

But, is such a call necessarily, plain and simple, an error in judgment? If this were so we would expect umpires to also show the same tendency in the opposite direction, i.e., calling runners safe who were in fact, out.

This question of judgmental bias has its origins in the earliest days of experimental psychology. Wilhelm Wundt (1832-1920) is generally credited with conducting the first psychological experiment. One of his interests centered on peoples' judgments of the timing of events when the events are "observed" through different sensory channels, e.g., auditory and visual channels. Simply put, his observations indicate, for example, that when one focuses more on an auditory event, e.g., a "click" than on a visual event, e.g., the location of a moving pendulum the "click" appears to occur fractionally earlier than is actually the case.

. I suspect that my reader is already ahead of me in seeing the parallel between Wundt's experiment and the job of first base umpires. Their task requires them to attend to the sound of the ball hitting the glove at the same time as they watch the runner's foot approach the bag. The only ingredient missing now to reproduce the conditions of Wundt's experiment is to have umpires attend more closely to the sound of the ball hitting the first baseman's glove. This, in fact, appears to be common practice. Advice in *The Umpire's Handbook* states:

> "The only way to make a call at first base is to watch the
> bag and listen for the sound of the ball hitting the glove
> of the fielder at first base. If you hear the ball hit the
> glove before the runner's foot hits the base, the runner is
> out. Otherwise, the runner is safe" (Brinkman & Euchner,
> 1987, p. 83).

All of this of course, leaves unanswered the question of whether this bias might also find its way into the calls of umpires in real life. Investigators at John Carroll University undertook to answer the question using a computer display that simulated a runner approaching first base with a burst of sound being emitted at points controlled by the researchers.

A group of 39 males who were certified umpires were recruited for the project. Another 39 students allowed for a comparison with a group of "non-experts". Having been reminded that the tie goes to the runner, all subjects individually judged a series of "close calls".

Recall if you will, that Wundt's finding would be found alive and well if umpires called more runners out who were in fact safe than those called safe who were in fact, out. Precisely this result was found. The comparison of umpires and students also produced a further surprise. Although the students showed the same tendency toward bias in their calls, they were found to be less susceptible than the umpires to this source of error.

The question is, why the difference? The investigators speculate that umpires have informally adopted a strategy of shortening games by calling runners out when the play is close. Although the practice represents a major departure from the official rules, the authors found support for their explanation in a survey of umpires. Fully one-quarter admitted that ties at first base did not go to "their" runners - they called them out!

31   The View from the Dugout

"If a woman has to choose between catching a fly ball and saving an infant's life, she will choose to save the infant's life without even considering if there are men on base"

Dave Barry

Baseball is one of a small number of sports in which a contest is made up of a series of discrete events, i.e., batters step up to the plate in turn, each facing a different set of circumstances. Managers for both teams are required to continually make tactical decisions throughout a contest. Should they intentionally walk the next batter? Should they call for a bunt or let the batter hit away? Should they have their runner attempt to steal second base? Each of these decisions is reached in the context of the game conditions prevailing at the time. Among the various factors to be taken into account are the inning, the score, the number of outs, positions of base runners, and the talent available on their rosters. Decisions made under these circumstances are potentially, enormously complex.

Now it must be said that the managers in a league are going to differ considerably in their abilities to make decisions of high quality or, put another way, decisions that more often benefit their team rather than harm their chances of a victory. Of course, managers everywhere, in business and industry, also have to make decisions on an ongoing basis that also affect the success of their group and the overall enterprise. However, baseball managers differ in one important respect. The result of each tactical decision is there for all the world to see. The runner was picked off trying to steal second; the bunt advanced a runner. By contrast, the wisdom of business managers' decisions is only partially revealed in the firm's monthly profit and loss statement.

Managers of professional teams generally have considerable experience, both as a player and as managers. It is this backlog of experience that they draw upon in formulating strategies and decisions. However, one must add aspects of the manager's personality to the mix. For example, are they inclined to be risk-takers or are they conservative decision-makers? However, despite this diversity in experience and personalities, the outstanding question for managers is how sound are the tactics they have historically employed? Have the decisions to walk the batter, steal second or bunt been tactics that succeed more often than they fail? Good answers are possible.

The very fact that the outcomes of managerial decisions are public and there for all to see opens the possibility of examining the success rates of various, managerial tactics. After all, the best way to arrive at answers to these questions is to see what has happened in the past in actual games. This has been done on at least one occasion using the records from a very large number of major league games. The conclusions from this research, some of which are listed below, should be seen as tentative and only apply to the average batter and/or the average runner. If you have a Mark McGwire or a Ricky Henderson at the plate or on base, these recommendations go out the window.

Intentional base on balls

Assuming a team of average batters, there is no evidence to support the tactic during games of giving an intentional walk in hopes of reducing the probability of the opposition scoring. Whether the tactic can potentially provide an advantage to the fielding team with "non-average" batters will depend on the skill of the batter coming to the plate and the batting averages of those following in the order. The tactic may however, be successful in the bottom of the ninth inning, albeit under specific circumstances. With the home team one run down and runners on second and third with one out, issuing an intentional walk increases the probability that they can win the game.

A further situation likely to increase the likelihood of a win is when the home team is in the field in the top of the ninth. This occurs when the score is tied, one out, and the visitors have runners at second and third. Under these conditions, a base on balls may pay off. However, in most circumstances in which the home team is leading, an intentional walk is ill-advised.

Sacrifice bunt

Typically, a bunt is attempted in hopes of advancing a runner from first to second base. Although the runner is likely to be thrown out at first, his teammate advances to second from where he can often score if a later batter singles. The chance of a double play thereafter is also thought to be reduced. The home team playing in the bottom of the ninth inning is advised not to lay down a bunt when they have a runner on first. A possible exception to this advice is when the score is tied and there are none out. For visitors in the top of the ninth with a runner on first, there are no circumstances where the probability of winning the game will be increased. The sacrifice is simply a bad tactic.

Stealing a base

Based on 5,016 instances in both major leagues in which players attempted to steal, 2,959 attempts or 58.8% were successful. Some individual players however, were considerably better than the average, enjoying success rates as high as 87%. Again assuming an "average" runner on first base, an attempted steal can be marginally more successful where a run is badly needed to gain a tie or to go one run up. However, it appears to be a failing tactic when a team is two or more runs down to their opponent. The decision to steal *late in the game* is more advisable when there is none out than when one is out. The tactic is clearly ill-advised with two out, the exception being when the team at bat is one run behind.

The foregoing represents only a smattering of the results that can be derived from the records of actual play. Moreover, they are based on the performances of hypothetical players having average skills at batting, stealing bases and bunting. Of course, similar calculations that take into account the superior (and inferior) skills of individual players could also be undertaken. However, the prospect of computers in the dugout holds little appeal for me and I suspect, the vast majority of fans. I think I prefer to see decisions made on the bases of intuition, hunches and experience however imperfect that process might be. Otherwise, most of the magic of the game will be lost.

As a footnote, I should emphasize that the conclusions described above are at best, tentative. The underlying calculations were based on major league play over 30 years ago. Much about the game has changed since then. Rules, the playing surface, equipment and personnel have all undergone changes over the years with the result that the same calculations based on current performance records may yield conclusions that are slightly or even totally different.[1]

---

[1] Baseball play-by-play databases are being developed on the following websites and offer the prospect of future research along the lines of that described above: <www.retrosheet.org> <www.baseball1.com> <www.baseballresearch.com>

32   Two Minutes Roughing... Make That Boarding

As we have seen in the previous section, the consistency of decision-making by ring officials is woefully inadequate. Boxing however, is not alone in this regard. In other sports where the action is fast-paced and frequently out of the officials' line of sight, we can expect that officials face similar difficulties. Ice hockey is one such sport.

When the official season records of 840 National Hockey League games were recently examined, the difficulties facing referees in trying to make sound (or reliable) calls became evident. As with boxing officials, the consistency in decisions across referees was to say the least, disappointing. Let me try to capture what might be occurring in the referee's mind in those few seconds when an infraction is taking place.

There is a scramble in the corner with perhaps as many as four or five players directly involved. In the midst of a great deal of pushing, poking and flailing about, there is a loud thump and a player falls to the ice. The crowd is screaming for a penalty to be called. From what he saw of the incident, it did not appear to the referee that the player accidentally stumbled or, took a dive. A penalty is obviously called for but, which one? In this and similar instances it could be any one of several rule infractions (e.g., boarding, cross-checking, elbowing, roughing). Although the details of what constitutes each of more than 20 penalties are carefully laid out in the "Rules of Play", the differences between some of them are slight. The added difficulties for referees is they often do not have a sufficiently clear view of what actually happened to accurately identify a specific penalty. Yet, a penalty of some sort must be called. It would appear that referees in these circumstances make their best guess as to which of several infractions was most clearly and seriously violated. Nonetheless, it is a highly subjective decision. Although they may appear supremely confident and decisive in their penalty call, referees apparently differ in their interpretations of the same event(s).

There are several means by which the reliability of decisions among referees might be increased. For example, some of the infractions that are highly similar in content might be combined through rule changes. In addition, the training of referees might focus on improving their agreement, i.e., inter-referee reliability, in making calls of the same infractions (perhaps videotaped). In the meantime, one referee's "roughing" is another referee's "boarding".

Summary

What is shown in the above sections are some of the limitations and biases attendant upon human decision makers. In some fast paced sports such as hockey, the demands placed on a referee are simply too great. Infractions occur in split seconds and are often beyond the referee's view. Being asked to identify specific infractions under such conditions may simply exceed the information processing abilities of even the most capable and experienced official.

In several chapters, biases were shown to creep into the decisions of judges, referees and umpires officiating at the highest levels of their sport. These are obviously not the result of inexperience. In fact, we might hazard the guess that at lower levels where officials are less highly trained and experienced, the margin of bias would be even greater.

At the same time, we are required to recognize that the structures of a majority of our sports does not easily lend themselves to electronic decision making devices. In any event, most people prefer the traditional ways of doing things and probably would not welcome changes to those arrangements even if it were possible. In many sports it is precisely the human element that makes the sport attractive to spectators. Still, in most cases, there is room for considerable improvement. With so much often riding on the outcome of competition, e.g., personal satisfactions, prestige and sometimes dollars, the ruling bodies of several sports might do well to consider taking steps to assist officials and coaches to improve the precision of their judgments.

VI. Myths Surrounding Sports

Introduction

My trusty Funk and Wagnalls dictionary defines myths as "any fictitious, or unscientific account, theory, belief, etc.". It is my impression that the sports world has more than its share of myths. People in all walks of life are constantly trying to make sense of the world around them. For the most part, they succeed. For example, we correctly observe that it is more difficult for a runner to steal second base with a left-hander on the mound. Or, under certain conditions, a "Hail Mary" pass is the play option most likely to snatch victory from defeat on the gridiron. These make sense to us and have stood the test of time. However, a number of other beliefs and practices that have grown up in sports have been found to be only partly true, or in some cases, just plain wrong.

Even so, it is recognized that myths perform several important functions in helping society meet the psychological needs of various social groups. Above all, they allow people to think they understand what is going on. That is, they believe they understand the "whys" of events occurring in their particular situation. It matters not whether the folklore/myth is true or false. In both cases, myths reduce feelings of uncertainty, provide a flow of information and establish a sense of order.

Each chapter in this section describes a myth that in some way touches sports. At the same time, I must accept the fact that many of the beliefs to follow are deeply held and are not easily laid to rest. As a consequence, I may be only partially successful in changing your views. After all, I can only pass on to you what competent researchers have found and leave it to you to accept or dismiss their findings. Their findings do however, represent the best available evidence on these questions.

33 Abner Doubleday and Cooperstown

The American version of baseball's origins was given official status by A. G. Spalding, a former star pitcher and later founder of the sporting goods company that still flourishes today. It was the decision of his blue ribbon panel in 1908 that baseball originated in the United States and that Abner Doubleday was its inventor. As baseball devotees know, the facts do not support either of the panel's conclusions.

As for Abner Doubleday, he was a Union artillery captain when the Confederate forces first fired on Fort Sumter at the start of the Civil War. He is credited with ordering the first volley in response to the Confederate attack. He later commanded troops at the battles of Antietam, Fredericksburg and Gettysburg, retiring with the rank of major general. However, there is no record of his ever being in any way linked to baseball. In the words of one historian, Abner Doubleday probably "didn't know a baseball from a kumquat".

Sports' most enduring myth is to be found in the origins of baseball. As the story goes, Abner Doubleday taught the game of baseball to a group of men who were playing marbles behind a tailor's shop in Cooperstown, New York in 1839. He explained the rules, sketched a diagram of the playing field and gave the new pastime the name "base ball" (spelled as two words). Today, as everyone knows, Cooperstown is the official home of baseball and site of the Hall of Fame. The small community boasts a baseball museum and library and hosts the annual induction ceremonies for the Hall of Fame.

The true origins of baseball undoubtedly lie in early 19th and 18th century England when a variety of stick and ball games were popular among the working class. Although they took various forms, they contained recognizable elements of the modern game. Indeed, one game played in the south of England was called "base ball". Because so much of the American psyche is invested in this delightful myth, we should perhaps not challenge it too forcefully.

34 Brainstorming: Are Two Heads Better Than One?

Sports generally require a great deal of planning and organization if they are to prosper. The unsung heroes who work behind the scenes spend countless hours in committees meeting one challenge after another. One of the more important challenges in today's economic climate is money. For most amateur organizations, their success rests on financial and other support from the general public and business community.

Imagine for the moment that your sport's executive has put you in charge of the annual fund raising campaign. Remembering the weak public response to last year's drive, it is apparent that some fresh new ideas are needed if the organization is to stay afloat. Fortunately, your job will be made easier by the half dozen dedicated and able people who will be working under you. What is needed are good ideas and lots of them. You decide to get your group together and brainstorm on the problem of how to raise money. Unfortunately, your first idea, i.e., to brainstorm, is a bad idea.

Brainstorming is more than a group of people getting together to work on solutions to a problem. Rather, a brainstorming session is conducted in accordance with a specific set of rules. Participants are encouraged to come up with as many ideas as they can and the "wilder" and more zany the suggestions the better. They are also encouraged to build upon the suggestions of others and to combine ideas. Most important, group members are instructed to withhold criticism of others' ideas. It is assumed that in this free-wheeling and accepting atmosphere groups will outdo individuals in producing both more and better quality ideas.

In virtually every sphere of human activity where creative solutions are needed, brainstorming has been embraced to the relative exclusion of an individualistic approach. Political, educational, military and business leaders have for nearly five decades consistently developed policy and programs based upon the results of brainstorming. However, evidence provided shortly after its general adoption in 1957 reveals in fact, that individuals working independently generate ideas of superior quality and overall, produce a greater number of ideas. Despite innumerable studies by social scientists, nearly all pointing to the same conclusion, leaders in various fields still cling tenaciously to the belief that decisions are better reached through group efforts. The truth is that they and the chairperson of our sports fund raising campaign might be more effective in their roles with solutions being sought on the basis of their group members working independently of one another.

There is little to be added to the general conclusion regarding brainstorming except perhaps, to ask why many organizations are so unshakable in their belief that people produce better ideas in groups than they do when working individually. We see for example, that following participation in brainstorming sessions, people are more satisfied with their contributions and enjoyed the experience more than those working individually. Moreover, irrespective of whether people have recently worked individually or in groups, fully 80% think that a person is more productive in a group situation. Why are people so convinced that two or more heads are better than one?

The basic reason underlying what has come to be called the **illusion of group effectivity** concerns an error in judgment. More specifically, individual participants in group brainstorming sessions tend to overestimate the number of ideas they contributed. Prompted by a tendency toward self-enhancement, individuals lay claim to ideas that in fact were proposed by others in the group. This overestimation of one's contribution arises from a difficulty in distinguishing between our own ideas and the ideas of others.

The next time you find yourself working with others on a major challenge that calls for creative solutions, it might be worthwhile to keep these findings in mind. Despite the appeal of brainstorming - it seems such a "democratic" way of doing things - better results are more likely to be realized in the long run with people working individually. This applies to our fund raising committee every bit as much as it does to decision making in other spheres of activity where creative solutions and ideas are needed.

35 That Ol' Devil Moon

Beliefs that the full moon can influence human behavior can be found in Shakespeare, the Bible, legal writings, folklore and music. Little wonder that a figure approaching two thirds of North Americans believe that at least some events are under lunar control. What follows is only a partial list of the behaviors thought to be open to influence: births, deaths, accidents, pyromania (fire setting), suicide, homicides, mental illness, epilepsy, aggression and lycanthropy (werewolves). However, for present purposes, we will focus on the popular assumption that interpersonal aggression is more likely to occur during the full moon phase of the lunar cycle.

Several investigations of a lunar-aggression link have been made using official records from ice hockey, a sport in which fights are commonplace. The researchers made every effort to tease out even a hint that the full moon might be related to aggression in the sport. Despite their best efforts and using the records from two full seasons of play, there was not the slightest indication of anything resembling lunar influence. Fights occurred irrespective of lunar cycles.

At the risk of disappointing believers even further, it must be said that those who have summarized the findings from all such studies have reached the same conclusion. Thus while it is true that murders follow a weekly cycle (peaking on weekends), there is no evidence to suggest that the phase of the moon is in any way involved, Neither I might add, do maternity wards get busy on nights of the full moon.

It may be instructive to look closely at the theory frequently offered to explain lunar influences by those who cling to the belief. Our attention is first drawn to the strong gravitational pull of the full moon in creating tides in large bodies of water. The explanation proposes that the same gravitational force acts in a similar fashion on the water content of our body. Thus, we are to imagine that during a full moon the water in each of our cells is sent sloshing this way and that driving us to commit homicide, suicide or, to starting fights.

The fallacy in this reasoning can be shown by the results of some straightforward calculations. The desk at which I am writing this book is exerting a gravitational pull on my body some 40,000 times greater than that exerted by the full moon. The reason of course, is that the full moon is at a vastly greater distance than my desk. While I must admit that I am sometimes driven to despair at my desk, I am not on those occasions gripped by homicidal or suicidal impulses nor by an uncontrollable urge to fight someone. Scientists do have a surprisingly good understanding of the causes of these destructive behaviors; lunar influence is not among the explanations. The answers are to be found in far more down-to-Earth explanations.

36 The Mars Effect

After the weather and sports, a favorite topic of discussion is the supernatural. When a conversation turns to astrology, horoscopes, charts, etc. skeptics in the group are quick to point out that there is not a shred of evidence to support the notion that the alignment of the planets at the time of our birth has anything to do with one's personality or the path one follows through life. At this point, one or more believers are apt to jump to the defence of astrology pointing to the Mars Effect as proof that astrology works. Thereafter, the discussion heats up.

What is the Mars Effect? At the risk of oversimplification, the path that Mars follows from sunrise to sunset is divided into 6 equal sectors (1 to 6) as is the time when it is below the horizon (7 to 12). The key sectors are 1 and 4, when Mars rises and when it crosses the north-south meridian, respectively. Based on extensive research by French psychologist Michel Gauquelin, a small but clear excess of outstanding, mainly French, sports champions appear to have been born at these times.

A variety of academics quickly surfaced to challenge Gauquelin's conclusions. Claims and counter-claims of methodological and design flaws in the original work and later replications flew back and forth. The arguments on both sides are extensive, detailed and often complex. I have waded into much of this literature and can only offer my humble opinion. For what it's worth, it does not appear to me that a case has been made for a surplus of top flight champions being born as Mars peeks above the horizon or stands due south. However, I have provided a sufficient number of references at the back of this book for those interested in following the debate and reaching their own conclusion.

This short chapter should trigger a connection in your mind with an earlier topic, the relative age effect (Chapter 2). Date of birth then, not time of birth, predicts to athletic success in some sports though not for reasons having anything to do with astrology.

37   We All Have our Ups and Downs

People have always had a strong interest in what the future holds for them. Will they be financially successful, travel to exotic countries, achieve fame, or meet that special someone? This fascination with seeing our futures or understanding and controlling the course of future events has been the energizing force behind an amazing array of occult practices. Tarot cards, astrology, palmistry, tea cup readings and psychics have at one time or another offered us a glimpse of the future and/or advice on matters of personal concern. The attraction that these practices hold for a segment of the population has supported a centuries-old industry that still thrives today in various forms, more recently under the umbrella of "New-age science".

A handful of these beliefs provide fairly specific predictions that can be tested by carefully controlled scientific research. For example, the claims made for the beneficial effects on mood of negative ions have not found support in the scientific community. Likewise, Chapter 35 on the effects of a full moon highlighted findings showing that fights in hockey games take place without regard for the phase of the moon. Another theory that reached its peak of popularity in the early 1980s is biorhythms. It too makes quite specific predictions that lend themselves to testing.

The theory of biorhythms originated with Wilhelm Fliess, a German nose and throat doctor and close friend for many years of Sigmund Freud. Described by one reviewer as a "world-class crackpot", Fliess's ideas included the proposition that the nose was closely related to neuroses and abnormal sexual conditions. Such ills were diagnosed by inspecting the interior of the nose and treated by cocaine applied to the "genital spots". In severe cases, part of the nasal bone might be removed to correct the condition. His other claim to fame is the subject of this chapter, namely, biorhythm theory.

The theory suggests that at the moment of birth three cycles are activated and repeat themselves, unchanging, throughout a person's lifespan. The first is a physical cycle of 23 days, the second an emotional cycle lasting 28 days and third, an intellectual cycle of 33 days duration. Knowing what phase a person is in allows one to make predictions regarding favorable or unfavorable days for engaging in various activities. During the positive or "up" phase of each cycle, a person's performance is thought to be superior whereas during negative or the "down" phase performance is thought to be worse than usual. "Critical" days occur when the rhythm is changing from a positive to negative phase or the opposite, negative to positive. On these days, performance is especially bad. Finally, there are the dreaded triple-critical days when all three cycles are simultaneously changing direction. On such a day, one is best advised to stay in bed.

Testing biorhythm theory in a sport is a fairly straightforward matter. All that is needed are the athletes' birthdates and their performance records from a reliable source. Not surprisingly, a substantial number of studies have been conducted in a variety of sports, all with essentially the same results. A sample of these studies reflects the overall pattern of findings on the question.

No-hitters are pitched with equal frequency on positive, negative and critical days. Golfers too, are just as likely to win tournaments on days that biorhythm theory would identify as critical. The days that pitchers die (a really down day) is equally likely to occur during positive and negative phases. Finally, winners and losers of heavyweight championship title bouts over three-quarters of a century (1899-1976) were indistinguishable on the basis of the theory.

By any standard, there is nothing to recommend biorhythm theory as having any value whatsoever in predicting how we, or the superstars of sport, will perform in future competitions. I might add that the theory is similarly unable to account for car accidents, academic achievement, death or recovery time following an operation. In short, while we all recognize that we have good and bad days, they are not fixed on the day we enter the world nor do they follow the course laid out by Dr. Fliess. We have our ups and downs for entirely different reasons.

Public enthusiasm for New-age information and paraphernalia has remained high in recent decades. As one fad emerges and later fades, another appears to take its place. The classified section of my (free) neighborhood newspaper lists advertisements for "palmistry healings", "aromatherapy", "thermal point therapy", "iridology", "intuitive massage", "raindrop therapy", "alien counselling", "glitializm" (body-mind immortality) and "Readings by Juliette" at the Magic Angel Cafe. The choices are endless.

Biorhythm was certainly big business in its heyday. Paperbacks, biorhythm calculators and kits produced enormous profits for the theory's promoters. However, this once thriving enterprise has faded in recent years. Although biorhythm charts continue to be published in the pages of a number of major newspapers, perhaps the results of scientific investigations such as those noted above may have finally trickled down and caused even diehard believers to lose interest.

38 Hi There! What's Your Blood Type?

The traditional opening gambit when men and women meet for the first time of "What's your sign?" may shortly be replaced by "What's your blood type?". A theory that blood type determines our personality has enjoyed widespread acceptance in Japan since World War II. Details of the notion have been published in some 30 books whose Japanese sales have exceeded 6 million copies.

Virtually everyone in Japan knows their blood type just as most North Americans know their astrological sign. Your blood type is believed to determine your success in matters of the heart, your financial future and your success in sports. The belief pervades all aspects of society. In advertising job vacancies, it is not unusual to find a statement to the effect that "only those with Type A or B blood should apply". Managerial decisions in Japanese major league baseball also take players' blood types into account.

Very simply, the theory identifies Type O individuals as born achievers, A's are seen to be deep thinkers, while B's are creative and Type AB's are problem solvers. More detailed personality descriptions are of course, available for each of the blood types. For example, in addition to being creative, Type B's are flexible, passionate, unconventional and have excellent concentration. Famous people are frequently cited as evidence for the theory, e.g., golfer Jack Nicklaus is Type B.

As fascinating as these notions are, it must be said that acceptable scientific evidence linking blood type to personality has been spotty at best. To quote one authoritative doubter, "blood type is about as relevant to personality as hair colour is to snorkeling ability" (Sullivan, 1996, p. 5).

Evidence of an association between blood types and athletic success was sought in the records of Japanese professional baseball. Blood types were obtained for 734 players, coaches and managers from Japan's Central and Pacific leagues. Success in the sport was examined from every angle. However, not even a hint of an association was uncovered.

◆ blood types did not differ among playing positions
◆ blood types did not differ between winning and losing teams
◆ blood types did not differ between winning and losing coaches/managers

Finally, the season leaders over nearly half a century were compared to the current crop of players. Historical title holders in home runs, runs batted in, pitching, earned run average and most valuable player performance categories were indistinguishable from those currently active on the basis of blood types.

At this point, there is nothing to suggest that a ballplayer's success is the result of their blood type. So, before coaches begin looking for an edge by recruiting athletes of a particular blood type, I would remind them that the advantage they gain will be about what would result from consulting astrological charts.

39 Not Tonight Dear, the Big Game is Tomorrow

A the risk of trying your patience, allow me a moment to stray somewhat from the topic at hand. Let me do so by raising a question. Is sex itself a sport? Considering that sexual activity involves the elements of skill, competence, healthy exercise and fun, it would appear to qualify as a sport every bit as much as other "officially" recognized activities. But you say, the element of competition is missing. Not necessarily. As one noted authority informs us, the Japanese historically staged something akin to a sexual Olympics. Let me cowardly sidestep your next question and leave it to your imagination to ponder details of the various events on the Olympic program.

An age old question for athletes and their coaches is whether sexual activity on the eve of a competition will hurt their performance. Judging from the actions of coaches in isolating athletes from their wives and girlfriends at training camp in preparation for championship competitions, we assume the belief is fairly widespread. The boxing fraternity in particular has historically kept women at arms length prior to important fights. Presumably, denying access to women results in a meaner and more aggressive fighter. The coach of the Costa Rican football team echoed this sentiment in banning his players from sexual activity until the conclusion of upcoming World Cup qualifying games. He is quoted as saying "I need all the players in full possession of their physical and mental faculties for the games against Mexico and the United States" ("No Sex Until, 1997). There is however, another point of view. The entire Italian national soccer team was taken to a brothel in preparation for their final 1994 World Cup match against Brazil. Need I tell you, they lost! (Brazil 3, Italy 2).

Notwithstanding the Costa Rican and Italian "experiments", researchers have in fact examined this question. Those who have taken up the question find no support whatsoever for the suggestion that performance factors such as strength, endurance, reaction time, etc. are in any way affected by earlier sexual activity. There is even a reasonable suggestion that sexual activity may instead, enhance later performance through a greater sense of well being.

How might a belief that sexual activity harms athletic performance have come into being in the first place? Its origins are almost certainly rooted in experience. Athletes and others have noted a connection between sex and poorer performances in competition. What is probably overlooked are the debilitating effects of alcohol and sleep-loss that often accompany the sex act. They alone could be responsible for any observed decline in performance. Sex by itself is unlikely to have any bearing on athletic prowess. However, a word of caution; sex at half-time is probably not a great idea!

Summary

In this section, we have looked at a number of commonly held beliefs that are in various ways related to sports. In each case we see that the best efforts of social scientists have thus far been unable to find evidence to support these beliefs. For the time being then, or until supporting evidence is found, they must be regarded as myths. Still, as I said at the top of the section, I recognize that for many people these beliefs are held with deep convictions and like superstitions, they are not easily changed. Of course, research is a continuing activity and it is always possible that a new study may yet turn up supporting evidence. In most areas of human behavior, we do not yet have anything resembling the final word.

VII. Near Myths

Introduction

The myths presented in the previous section are clearly that, myths. There is not a shred of supporting evidence available. Abner Doubleday did not invent the game of baseball, two heads are not better than one and your life is not determined at the moment of your birth. We now turn to a collection of topics that are likely to be myths, what I have called "near myths". They qualify as near myths only because we cannot be entirely certain as to their falsity. Either studies attesting to the mythical status of the belief are few in number or there is something less than a consensus of opinion in the scientific community.

40 Sport Widows

> *If a man watches three football games in a row,*
> *he should be declared legally dead*
> Erma Bombeck (1927-1986).

We are all familiar with the stereotype of the sports widow. She is that long-suffering and neglected woman who keeps her significant other supplied with chips and beer while he watches endless hours of sports programming. He in turn, is an unshaven, pot-bellied, couch potato with little or no time for his wife, children and his household responsibilities.

If women are truly suffering as a result of their man's passion for sports, countless relationships are imperiled. But how do women feel about the quality of their romantic relationships when they find their husbands or boyfriends camped on the couch, away at the ball park or off coaching Little League?

The question was recently put to large samples of women in Indianapolis and San Diego, both cities boasting professional sport franchises. Women said overwhelmingly that involvement in sports by the men in their lives had a positive influence on their relationship.

Two studies conducted at the University of Lethbridge produced similar results. Both a sample of coeds involved in romantic relationships and a sample of women from across Alberta were asked for their views. While 55% thought their man's involvement in sports had no effect on the strength of their relationship, 35% felt the relationship had improved as a result. Only 10% believed that an interest in sports had weakened their relationship. However, there was an interesting twist to these findings.

At the time of the interviews the women also completed a measure that assessed the actual closeness of their relationships. From the foregoing, one would predict that those with mates consumed by sports would have the closest relationships. Surprisingly, such was not the case. There was no relationship between the extent of mens' involvement in sports and the strength or closeness of their relationships.

It is difficult to reconcile these discrepant findings. That is, on the one hand women report that sports have generally strengthened their relationships but on the other hand, there is no evidence of this when the strength of the relationship is formally assessed. One suggestion among several would allow that "love is blind".

41   Pitching Illusions

"A pitch can curve, wobble or dip but it doesn't hop or break". The reference here is to baseball's rising fastball and breaking curveball. More to the point, does a (rising) fastball actually rise or hop or, is it simply an illusion? Similarly, does a breaking curveball actually "break" and drop in the last few feet or again, are batters victims of a perceptual illusion?

Long before baseball began, scientists pondered the dynamics of the curveball. Sir Isaac Newton (1642-1727) of gravity fame described the aerodynamics of the tennis ball that can be made to curve. The spin put on the ball by the racquet causes unequal air pressure on opposite sides of the ball forcing it to follow a curved path. The same explanation has been applied to the curveball in baseball. However, other pitches such as the slider and knuckleball also take erratic trajectories. For example, the slider is faster than a curveball and only begins to curve as it nears the plate. The knuckleball has little or no spin on it and changes direction, sometimes more than once, before reaching the plate. These influences on the path of the pitch are caused by turbulence produced in the wake of the ball.

By way of illustration, consider the sideview in the Figure below (Chapman, Bahill & Wymore, 1992, p. 338. Reprinted by permission)[2] that shows the air flow around a "spinning baseball". Note that the air flows evenly around the ball until it reaches what are called the separation points. Thereafter, the air flow is caught up in a chaotic, swirling air mass, i.e., the wake. The effect of the spin is to create more friction on the top of the ball thus shifting the wake. This downward pressure will cause the ball to drop more than it would without spin. Now, look at this same Figure as if it was a view of the ball from above. The separation points marking the edges of the wake are shifted such that the sideways force instead produces a curved trajectory for the pitch.

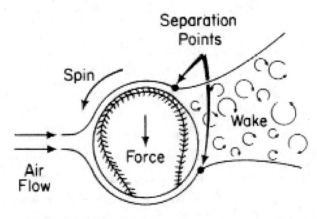

Those who have studied baseball pitches in wind tunnels with sophisticated

---

[2] Chapman, W., Bahill, A., & Wymore, W. (1992). *Engineering Modeling and Design,* Boca Raton, FL: CRC Press.

photographic technology over the past three decades are well satisfied that numerous erratic trajectories can occur. The patterns of turbulence creating these trajectories are determined by, (1) ball spin and, (2) the velocity of the pitch. However, they are equally in agreement that the fast ball does not rise nor hop for that matter, and the curveball does not suddenly break.

The fastball: Although backspin on a pitch will cause the ball to drop more slowly than it otherwise would, there is nothing to suggest that it could rise against the downward pull of gravity. There is also nothing to suggest that it could accelerate and hop over the bat (batters report "hops" of up to 1 ft). Indeed, the best that humans have been able to do is to impart a spin producing a force equal to only two-thirds that of gravity. So while the fall may be lessened considerably with sufficient backspin, it does not rise.

The curveball: The curveball similarly obeys all known laws of physics. The spin causes the ball to curve. If the spin is horizontal, the ball will curve horizontally. If the ball is given topspin, then it will drop more sharply than it would if gravity was the only downward force acting on it. The laws of physics and all the evidence says that a curve is continuous and does not break as it nears the plate.

Yet, batters will swear that they have seen both types of pitches with their own eyes, a hop in the first instance and a break in the second. No one doubts they have. The illusion is real; that is the nature of illusions. For reasons that involve the inability of batters to continuously follow the ball with their eyes for the entire distance from the mound to the plate, and, misjudging the speed of the pitch, the illusion of an erratic trajectory results.

Still, I recognize that some will continue to believe what their own eyes have told them, especially ball players who have been victimized by a "rising" fastball. Chronic doubters may take some comfort in the knowledge that it can be shown by analyses applying the same aerodynamic principles that bumblebees cannot fly! While there may still be room for argument on exactly how the illusion arises, it does appear that "rising" and "breaking" are creations of our perceptual systems.

42 Batting Under Pressure

It is generally recognized in sport psychology circles that athletes performing a complex or difficult task show a decline in performance in situations that are highly arousing. Inasmuch as most batters are successful on less than 30% of their trips to the plate, batting qualifies as a difficult task. As such, measures of individual batting proficiency would be expected to show a decline in pressure-packed situations.

Baseball players can experience high levels of stress in a variety of circumstances. One particularly stressful time for a player is the weeks or months prior to being traded when rumors of a trade are swirling in the media and around the league. Players generally would prefer not to be traded and feel pressured to improve their performance and stave off a move to a new team.

Two other pressure situations occur within games. Late inning pressure is felt by batters coming to the plate in the late innings of a close game with runners in scoring position. Batters also feel extra pressure at the plate at any point in a game when there are two outs with a runner(s) on base. Several studies have examined the effects of pressure-packed situations on batting proficiency. In these studies batting performance was represented by the traditional batting average as well as a slugging average that additionally took into account the number of bases resulting from a hit, i.e., power hitting. In all of these pressure situations -- waiting to be traded, coming to the plate in the late innings of a close contest and, with two outs and runners on base -- batting performance was worse than when players batted in non-pressure circumstances.

Perhaps, the most intriguing result of all questions a common tactic, that of sending in an older, more experienced player to bat in pressure-packed situations. The idea has always been that the seasoned veteran has somehow habituated or is immune to these external pressures. Not so! The declines in batting performance did not differ between the younger and older players nor between those with limited experience and the grizzled veterans. When the going gets tough, just put in your best hitter.

43　When You're Hot, You're Not

Time for a pop quiz.

Question #1. What follows are the results of two coin tossing exercises. As you might expect, the results are random. Actually, I am lying. I have fiddled with one of the sequences and made it non-random. Is it sequence (a) or sequence (b) that is a random distribution of heads and tails?

(a) HTHHTTHHTHTHHT　　　　　　(b) HTTTTTHHTHLHHTHT

Question #2. You have been watching a series of coin tosses that so far have produced the following sequence of heads and tails.

THHTHTTHTHTTHTTTTT__? Assuming the toss is entirely fair and the coin is not in any way biased, would you predict that the next toss will be a head or a tail?

If you chose (a) as the sequence that represents a completely random pattern, then you join a majority of people who misperceive random sequences. If you chose (b), take a bow. What is operating here is a strong cognitive illusion that leads us to anticipate more alternations in a series than would in fact occur on a random basis. Put another way, our understanding of what is random does not allow for extended runs, as seen in choice (b). When we see streaks of this sort, we no longer see their occurrence as part of a random process. Having rejected the notion that the series is random, we then look elsewhere for an explanation. As we will see momentarily in regard to basketball, sportscasters, coaches and fans alike see streaks in the performances of players and credit them with having "the hot hand" or being a "streak shooter". In truth, nothing of the sort is taking place. What is being observed is the operation of an entirely chance process.

Before proceeding however, let us look at Question #2 that illustrates another powerful cognitive illusion. The answer is that H and T are equally likely to occur. Nonetheless, a majority of people invariably choose heads. Known as the gambler's fallacy, the reasoning is that heads are overdue, that the odds of a head on the next toss have been building up. Indeed, people assume consciously or unconsciously, that the next toss will somehow be influenced by the previous tosses. What is not commonly recognized is that coin tosses are completely independent events. Coins do not have memories of past events, opinions on last night's game or, plans for the future. With each toss the odds remain 50-50 that heads will occur. Even knowing all of this, many will still cling to the belief and answer Question #2 "heads".

Returning to Question #1, the cognitive illusion it represents lies behind the widely held belief that basketball players have the hot hand or are streak shooters in some games. However, different people mean different things when they speak of the hot hand. With this in mind, Thomas Gilovich of Cornell University along with colleagues Robert Vallone and Amos Tversky of Stanford undertook to investigate versions of the hot hand hypothesis. Answers were sought in the playing records of the Philadelphia 76ers of the National Basketball Association.

One version suggests that having just made their last shot (or several shots in a row) the likelihood of players hitting on the next shot is greater than when they just missed the previous shot (or several shots in a row). Regardless of whether one considers one or several shots in a row, the probability of a hit on the next shot following a hit was found to be, if anything, slightly lower than following a miss. The overall trend actually runs counter to the belief that players have the hot hand in shots from the floor.

Another interpretation of the hot hand sees players having "hot" or "cold" nights on the floor. Players' total points will of course, differ from game to game. The question becomes whether there are major departures from their individual averages that are any greater than would be expected by chance alone. The authors summarize their findings on this question as "...indicating that variations in shooting percentages across games do not deviate from their overall shooting percentage enough to produce significantly more hot (or cold) nights than expected by chance" (Gilovich et al., 1985, p. 302).

Perhaps the hot hand will reveal itself at the free throw line? A belief in this possibility is strong among knowledgeable fans. Told that a particular player has a 70% success rate from the free throw line, fans were asked to estimate the likelihood that he would hit on the second of two free throws having just hit on the first. They saw the hit on the first shot as increasing the likelihood of a hit on the second shot. A second question asked fans to estimate the likelihood that this same player would hit the second free throw having missed the first. Having missed the first free throw, the player was thought to be less likely to hit on the second shot.

The actual performance of the 76ers however, did not justify the fans' beliefs. Following a hit on their first shot, they were slightly less likely than would be expected from their averages to hit on the second. Conversely, a miss on the first was slightly more likely to be followed by a hit, all of which runs counter to the hot hand hypothesis. Thus, regardless of how the "hot hand" is interpreted, i.e., hot streaks, hot nights or hot shots from the free throw line, it simply fails for support when real life basketball records are examined.

I am not so naive as to believe that I have convinced most of my readers, especially basketball fans, that the hot hand is a myth. My own experience tells me otherwise. The first time I presented the topic to my sports psychology class, I anticipated they would be enthralled and have a profound learning experience as I systematically went about unravelling a sports fallacy. The lecture was an utter failure. While I was given a polite hearing, the students initial disbelief gradually gave way to even more disbelief in the findings (mind you, they took notes and produced "correct" answers on their exam). However, audible comments to the effect that Gilovich and his colleagues didn't know basketball and several muffled guffaws from the back row convinced me that few were persuaded by my arguments. I might have had more success convincing them that Gilovich and company had recently uncovered evidence that the Earth after all, is flat. My puny case was up against a lifetime of eyewitness evidence of sequenced events that appear to be anything but random. Such is the power of cognitive illusions.

44 Momentum: On a Roll or Not?

Perhaps the most overworked word used by broadcasters describing events at the 2000 Summer Olympics was "momentum". But they are not alone. Athletes, coaches, fans and media analysts too have unreservedly embraced the concept to explain the ebb and flow of competition. Momentum takes on a variety of forms and is known by several names, a.k.a. "the hot hand" (see the previous chapter), streak shooting, "on a roll", a slump (negative momentum), etc. Furthermore, it is presumed to operate at both the individual and team performance levels as well as within a single contest or over an entire season of play.

There seems little doubt that athletes and others perceive that momentum exists and frequently cite its influence in accounting for an athlete or team surging ahead in a contest. Alternatively, individuals or teams may lose momentum as their rival enjoys a run of success.

A number of early studies in racquetball and tennis produced results that seemingly showed psychological momentum at work. Players winning the first game were more likely to go on to win the next game or match. But is this really evidence of momentum? It might be if the competitors paired in these matches were of equal ability.

Consider the situation in which Pete Sampros is persuaded to play a match against the author. To no one's surprise, Mr. Sampros wins the first game (40-0) and shortly thereafter the first set (6-0). In fact, he scarcely breaks a sweat in winning the entire match (6-0, 6-0). Did Mr. Sampros triumph over the author for reasons having anything to do with his acquiring momentum with his win in the first game, or set? Hardly! Unless the ability of the competitors (or teams) is taken into account, we would be naive to infer the existence of momentum simply from early success.

The notion of momentum also features prominently in the jargon of those describing the rise and fall of teams in league play. Successive wins are seen to be examples of momentum at work while prolonged slumps in team performance prompt calls for measures to snap the losing streak, to get back on track and regain momentum. While many in the sporting community strongly believe that momentum is an underlying force responsible for the changing fortunes of teams, evidence of its existence has not been forthcoming. As with its close cousin, "the hot hand", momentum has proved to be elusive.

Consider a study carried out at the level of professional team sports. The patterns of winning and losing were examined for 28 major league baseball teams across the 1996 season. A similar examination was made of the records of 29 National Basketball Association teams over the 1996-'97 and 1997-'98 seasons. Careful analyses failed to uncover evidence that wins and losses are in any way the result of previous game outcomes. Momentum has also been credited with building extended winning (and losing) streaks. Again, it is the same story. The lengths of winning and losing streaks were no longer than would be expected by chance. The current status of momentum is captured in the words of the researcher whose work I have described. He notes "... one is strongly tempted to conclude that while momentum is widely accepted as a phenomenon by sport participants, fans and observers, it is more myth than reality" (Vergin, 2000, p. 195). It would appear that its effects on performance, if any, are at best trivial.

45   Icing the Shooter

Basketball games are frequently won or lost at the free throw line. By one estimate, approximately 20% of all points are scored at the free-throw line. Additionally, for both winning and losing teams, free-throws comprise a higher percentage of total points in the last 5 minutes of a game than they do in the early part of a contest. Perhaps not suprisingly, winners score more points at the free-throw line than losers. The success of penalty shots in the late stages of a contest then, is often decisive in determining the outcome.

One of the options available to a coach is to call a timeout. Over the years a very popular tactic has been to bring a stoppage in play just before an opposing player attempts a free throw (by one estimate, approximately 94% of Division II coaches use this tactic). The same tactic is also used in football. With time running out, coaches often call a timeout just as the opposing team lines up to attempt a game-winning field goal.

Sometimes referred to as icing, the practice assumes that the player's performance will somehow cool down, he will lose his concentration or become increasingly anxious over the prospect of missing the upcoming shot in a critical game situation. Coaches have assumed that with time to reflect on the consequences of failure, the added stress on the shooter increases the likelihood of a miss. Certainly, we know that extremely high levels of arousal or anxiety are generally associated with poorer performance. But is that actually happening at the free throw line?

An examination of NCAA Division I men's basketball records produced a surprising result. The records in question were those of eight teams competing in the Southwest, Western Athletic and Big Sky conferences from 1977 to 1989. In all, 1,237 games were analyzed. Of free-throw attempts that were not preceded by a timeout, 68.7% were successful. However, of all free-throws attempted after a timeout was called, 73.4% were successful. The difference is in just the opposite direction to the reasoning underlying coaches' justification for using the tactic.

Just a word about the difference between 68.7% and 73.4%. While it is impressive, the difference falls just short of being statistically significant and as a consequence must be regarded as due to chance. However, what can be said about the tactic of calling timeouts prior to free throws is that to this point the practice is not supported by the available evidence. At the same time it is reasonable to also question the wisdom of icing the field goal kicker in football. By way of explanation, it has been suggested that any increase in the shooter's anxiety is more than offset by the rest and opportunity to gain composure that is provided by the timeout. It would appear at this point that the tactic of calling timeouts is overdue for a major re-think.

46 Jockeys, Gender and Dollars

There is only a handful of professional sports in which men and women compete against each other. Even then, such events are held only occasionally and/or at irregular intervals. Women have qualified for a place in the starting lineup at the Indianapolis 500 car race. For decades, others have acquitted themselves well against men in long distance swimming. In recent years women have won Alaska's grueling 1,169 mile Anchorage to Nome Ididyrod dog sled race. It seems then that in those few activities where authorities have sanctioned competition between the sexes, women have performed at least on a par with males. However, two professional activities in particular stand apart from all others in allowing men and women to compete on a regular basis, i.e., show jumping and more recently, thoroughbred racing.

The question of whether women can compete successfully against men in equestrian events is answered in the title of a study appearing in the *Journal of Recreational Mathematics*: "Are women the weaker sex in Grand Prix jumping? The answer is nay". In fact, the authors found that over a season of jumping females earned more points and more prize money on the circuit than male riders.

Yet another study has examined the success of female jockeys in thoroughbred horse racing. But first, it should be noted that only 13% of all jockeys riding on US thoroughbred race tracks are women. They seemingly face a number of discriminatory barriers in the male-dominated sport. The result is that the purse money claimed by male riders is nine times that of females. Moreover, males ride in twice as many races as females, a fact that significantly reduces the total winnings of females. Yet despite these obstacles, it was found that "holding performance, experience, and the number of mounts constant, the model predicts a significant winnings differential in favor of women riders" (Ray & Grimes, 1993, p. 59).

Success in the sport can however, be measured in other than monetary terms. Quite apart from the total purses women earn, how do female jockeys fare against male riders in getting their mounts to the wire? Here we are asking about possible sex differences in sheer riding ability. In the words of the authors' "...holding everything else constant, women appear to be outperforming men at the finish line" (Grimes & Ray, 1995, p. 103).

Two studies -- even ones as competently conducted as these -- seldom tell the whole story. For now however, it appears that the racing track is not level for women riders and given opportunities, they can at least match the performance of male jockeys. Overall, in those sports where stature and brawn are not essential for success, women can likely hold their own in competition with men.

47 NFL Myths

> *Football isn't a contact sport; it's a collision sport*
> *Dancing is a contact sport*
> Vince Lombardi (1913-1970)

Media analysts have observed that National Football League commentators routinely emphasize three aspects of performance that they see as essential to a winning season. First, winning teams have a strong running game. Second, the running and passing aspects of the game are related to each other. That is, if a team has a successful running game, they should also have a superior passing game. Third, the record of fumbles and fumble recoveries are an indication of a team's strength or power. How valid are these beliefs?

Early evidence assessing the importance of various offensive aspects of the game was based on the records of the 28 NFL teams competing during the 1991 season. Essentially, all teams were found to be equally adept at running the ball, averaging approximately four yards per rush. Contrary to popular belief, the yardage of teams winning at least nine out of sixteen games did not differ from those with losing seasons.

Support for the belief that yardage gained by rushing is related to yardage gained by passing also failed to find support in the official records of play. For example, if teams excelled in their passing game, there was simply no indication that their ground games also tended to be superior. Finally, do stronger teams have fewer fumbles and more fumble recoveries than weaker teams? Apparently not! Again, teams with a winning season did not differ in this regard from those with a losing season.

What aspect of play does set winning teams apart from losing teams? One answer appears to be interceptions. Teams that intercept a greater number of passes than they have intercepted by their opponents typically end the season on a winning note. The defense then appears essential to a successful season. But overall, just how important is the defense -- compared to the offense -- in producing victories?

Recent studies suggest that the play of the defense completely overshadows that of the offense in predicting a winning season. When recent seasons of regular NFL games were examined two performance measures stood out above all others in predicting success. The first is the turnover differential, described by Onwuegbuzie (2000) as "... the difference between the number of fumbles and interceptions gained by a team's defense and the number of fumbles and interceptions given away by the same team's offense" (p. 641). The second is the total number of rushing yards conceded by the defense, a measure directly reflecting a team's ability to "stop the run". These two measures alone eclipse in importance several lesser indicators, e.g., percentage of third-down plays that resulted in a first down, total number of passing first downs attained by the offense. Seemingly, we are looking in the wrong place for the secret to a winning season.

Incidentally, a similar examination was also made of a regular season of National Basketball Association games. In the case of basketball, it appears that it is the *offensive* skills of teams that are more important to winning. Of all the performance measures used, it was the three point conversion percentage that proved to be the best predictor of success.

48 Morality on the Links

The setting was the 2nd round of the 1925 US Open played at Worcester, Massachusetts. One of golf's greatest players, Bobby Jones found himself in the rough at the side of the green. He grounded his club to play a little lob shot. The ball moved. Jones stepped back. No one saw the ball move, not the caddies, not the officials, not his playing partner, Walter Hagen. Jones immediately called a penalty on himself. His double bogey 6 and his round of 77 put him in danger of missing the cut and with it, any hope of winning the Open. However, a 70 the following day put him back in contention and he went on to tie for the championship. He lost to Willie Macfarland in a playoff by a single stroke.

Later, an Associated Press interviewer commended Jones for his honesty. Jones however, saw nothing particularly commendable in what he had done replying "You might as well praise me for not robbing banks" (Sommers, 1995, p. 82). Such is the measure of the man.

Just how honorable are those of us who play the grand old game? Is it a relatively rare event when golfers cave in to the pressures to score well and resort to cheating? Perhaps the temptations are greatest when playing alone or in a twosome where the chances of rule violations are less likely to be detected by others? Maybe instead, when we are part of a larger group, i.e., a foursome, it somehow brings out the worst in us?

Researchers sought answers to these and other questions by observing 150 golfers as they played the first hole of a public golf course. Observations were made from a hidden vantage point on a second-storey balcony above the first fairway. Observations made at different times of the day over a five-day period revealed that fully 75/150 (50%) of the golfers violated at least one United States Golf Association (USGA) rule. Of these, 14 violated two rules while 2 players violated 3 rules in the course of playing the first hole.

Easily the most common violation was players conceding putts to themselves, a total of 50 players rewarding themselves in this way. A further 22 golfers found it necessary to improve their lie while 6 played two balls simultaneously. Finally, five who were apparently unhappy with their shots simply replayed them.

Those breaking the rules tended to be the less skilled golfers. Moreover, the size of the playing group was also related to rule violations. That is, the larger the group the more rule violations were in evidence. By way of explanation, it is suggested that group norms stressing improved performance act as a source of pressure to violate the constitutive rules of the game. These pressures to improve their play would presumably be stronger and more in evidence as the size of the playing group increased.

Incidentally, it is noteworthy that agreements among players to establish normative rules that conflict with the USGA constitutive rules is itself a violation. Finally bear in mind that rule violations were tallied only for the first hole - another 17 holes remained to be played! By a rough calculation using the first hole as typical of those remaining in the round, the sample of golfers committed a total of approximately 1,581 (93 x 17) additional rule violations before they reached the clubhouse.

Summary

The near myths in this section are in some ways more intriguing than the full-fledged myths described earlier. While the evidence to date points to their mythical status, there is still room for lively debate and differences of opinion. For this reason, I have left the door open - just a crack. Who knows! One or more of these beliefs may yet find support in the scientific community.

VIII. Sports Heroes and Records

ACTS OF WORSHIP

If you're too much in awe, you'll never love this game. Sooner or later, you've got to hit Gordie and flatten him if you can the way Henry Moore used to have his kids piss on each of his sculptures when they were done to show they were, after all, only things. Of course you can't. Gordie is just too strong. But if you're lucky he'll give you an elbow behind the ref's back and you'll see what a bastard he is. That'll cure you.[3]

Richard Harrison

from: *Hero of the Play*

Introduction

There is no shortage of candidates for hero status. Virtually every sport can provide an array of outstanding athletes either from an earlier era or from among those still actively competing. Many have been enshrined in Halls of Fame with a view to keeping alive the flickering memories of past achievements for future generations.

Although outstanding athletes are plentiful and can potentially serve as role models for aspiring youngsters, the personal qualifications of many are suspect. Recent years have seen too many would-be heroes fall from grace. With disturbing regularity we learn of star athletes being involved with illegal drugs, gambling, domestic violence and an assortment of other criminal activities. What is sorely needed are standards for distinguishing between true heroes and others who lack the requisite qualities.

One such set of standards has been offered by Robert Barney and is presented

---

[3] Gordie Howe (NHL Hall of Fame)

briefly below.[4] It is a set of criteria that might be kept in mind inasmuch as the chapters in this section deal solely with outstanding performers with little attention being given to their personal qualities.

◆ First, and not surprisingly, the athlete must represent physical excellence.

◆ Second, they must display moral excellence in all aspects of their lives, i.e., traits such as honesty, humility, generosity, sportsmanship and self-control.

◆ Third, the candidate for hero status must give unselfishly of their energies and talents to assist others less fortunate than themselves.

◆ Fourth, the individual must exhibit theoretical and practical wisdom, e.g., show responsibility in dealing with personal decisions regarding money, alcohol, gambling, etc.

◆ Finally, true hero status should not be accorded an athlete in his/her lifetime. The sheer passage of time may bring a more objective and balanced perspective to bear on a candidate's qualifications.

Of course, the above standards represent an ideal that most candidates for hero/heroine status only approach. While their achievements may be worthy of admiration, it is their personal qualities that should form the bases for adopting them as role models, heroes, etc. Barney's criteria represent a starting place for parents and others to consider and may allow us to avoid placing inferior role models before our children.

---

[4] Barney, R. K. (1985). The hailed, the haloed, and the hallowed: Sport heroes and their qualities-An analysis and hypothetical model for their commemoration. In N. Muller & J. Ruhl (Eds.), *Sport history* (pp. 88-103). Niederhausen, Germany: Schors-Verlag.

49   Sport Heroes as Agents of Change

At one time or another most of us have been dazzled by the skills of a Michael Jordan, Wayne Gretsky, Steffi Graf or Maradona. A single brilliant moment (e.g., Sir Roger Bannister's four-minute mile), or an outstanding career (e.g., pitcher, Nolan Ryan) can bestow superstar status on an athlete. The media attention, the critical acclaim and lavish rewards that result from their achievements all but ensure them a special place in the memories, indeed, the everyday conversations of their admirers. It takes only a small step to conclude that their status and prestige makes them ideal candidates to serve as role models for those who admire them. As such we might also assume that they are in a position to influence their fans in positive ways.

Community leaders across North America have acted on these assumptions and established innumerable programs whereby it is hoped that outstanding athletes can exert a positive influence on admirers. Popular athletes talk to students about the importance of staying in school, give motivational speeches to drop-outs, lend their name and energies to fund raising drives and, urge people to avoid drugs and practice safe sex in an era of AIDS. Other more commercially-minded athletes endorse a range of products from breakfast cereals, to jockey shorts to feminine hygiene products.

The logic of these programs draws a measure of support from attitude change experiments. In the short run at least, high status or prestigious communicators are generally effective in changing the attitudes of an audience in the desired direction. There is always a further question however, if whether having changed an attitude it necessarily results in a corresponding change in behavior. After all, it is usually a change in behavior that is the actual goal of the entire enterprise. That is, do the admirers actually stay in school, donate money, practice safe sex or buy jockey shorts? It is this question that lies at the heart of what is called program evaluation research.

I must admit that when I first thought about this question some years ago, it seemed obvious to me that athletes serve as effective role models for a majority of our youth and that when they give advice people listen and many take their advice. Now, I'm not so sure. Let me tell you why I have serious doubts that the superstars of sport are any more than marginally better able than others to shape public attitudes and behaviors.

First off, almost a century of intermittent research on people's heroes, exemplars, or role models indicates that sports figures represent a very minor category. In one US national poll of adults conducted over a period of 37 years, less than 1% mentioned a sportsperson as someone they most admire. Other surveys have found that athletes represent approximately 11% of youngsters' choices. Despite indications that a whopping majority of Americans describe themselves as sports fans and actually participate in sports or keep fit activities, it must be said that they do not draw their personal heroes from the sportsworld in large numbers. Our heroes appear instead, to be drawn from among our friends and relatives, easily the largest category. These are not the people then, who make the headlines or appear on the evening news. As for their influence, girls are more influenced by their friends and relatives than by sport and entertainment figures. Boys on the other hand report being influenced more by relatives and entertainment personalities than by exemplars chosen from among their friends or sport figures.

The second reason for my doubting that star athletes are all that more effective than others arises from a study evaluating the impact of Magic Johnson's announcement of his HIV infection. On November 7, 1991 Johnson announced to the world that he had tested positive for the AIDS virus. The intense media coverage of his press conference and his later efforts on behalf of national campaigns to educate the public were presumed to have made people more aware of the personal risks they face as well as provide a greater understanding of the disease and how it is transmitted.

Late in the summer of 1991, John Sumser of California State University at Stanislaus administered a questionnaire asking students about the sources of AIDS infection, e.g., blood donations, the dentist's office, and the likelihood that they would get infected. Three weeks after Johnson's press conference, the questionnaire was again administered to the students. Somewhat surprisingly, there was no apparent change in students' ratings of personal risk nor were they any better informed on the topic. Of course, the possibility remains open that specific subgroups (e.g., young, urban Blacks, "media and policy elites") may have been influenced by Johnson's message.

To return to the original question, i.e., my doubts regarding the effectiveness of superstars to educate and change the day to day behaviors of the general public, two points have increased my skepticism. The category of sports is very small, especially for females, and such evidence as we have does not give me cause for optimism. Probably no comparable event in recent history has been given such widespread and intense media attention and involved such a charming and likable person. It is hard to imagine a more persuasive individual. Yet, the students at Stanislaus held firmly to their beliefs. As a footnote, what Sumser did find to be effective in changing attitudes/behaviors regarding AIDS is personally knowing someone who has become infected. That seems to strike home!

Still, I must acknowledge that other assessments of the impact of Magic's announcement have shown an influence on people's attitudes and at least some aspects of their behavior. Interviews with men waiting to ride on Chicago's mass transit system revealed an increased concern that an "acquaintance" will get AIDS but that concern remained unchanged for them personally as did their perceived risk of contracting the disease. However, among Blacks in the sample, concern about the subject of AIDS did rise following Magic's disclosure. Also, both racial groups sought more information on AIDS and were more likely to discuss the topic with friends in the future.

Of course, it might be hoped that Magic Johnson's dramatic announcement would have an even stronger impact on youngsters. In a study involving Black junior high school students in Cleveland, the results were in some ways puzzling. While they wanted to know more about the disease following the announcement, other findings were contrary to those predicted by the researchers. For example, students saw themselves as less likely to become infected with the AIDS virus and, were more anxious about interacting with an AIDS victim after the announcement. Because worries about the disease have been linked to changes in sexual behavior that reduce the risk, the fact that students worried less following the announcement is disheartening. After all, the ultimate goal of celebrity speakers generally is to change some aspect of their audience's behavior, in this case, their sexual practices.

There was somewhat better news at the University of Florida. Students were asked to imagine that a graduate student who had contracted the HIV virus through a blood transfusion was in desperate need of help with a class project. Were he to fail the course, he would be required to drop out of school. Specifically, the grad student needed help in stuffing envelopes and making phone calls as part of a survey he was conducting. The response of males to his appeal was enthusiastic. Fully 83% of the men volunteered to assist one week after the announcement in stark contrast to zero% just before Magic's disclosure. Among women, 63% were already volunteering their help prior to the announcement, a level that remained unchanged. In this instance, Magic may in effect have been preaching to those already converted. However, on another measure, i.e., the amount of time they would volunteer, these same women showed an increase from before to after the announcement. The gain in altruism resulting from Magic's announcement gradually declined over the next four and a half months to about 32% overall. Still, we should be thankful for any gains realized on this and other health issues, however short-lived they may be.

One explanation among several is to be found in the results of consumer research. As noted above, there is a widespread assumption that media and sports celebrities are highly effective as spokespersons for various products and causes. The presence of a celebrity seen as *physically attractive* and/or *trustworthy* is generally thought to prompt us to purchase products and/or support a cause. Magic rates high on both characteristics. However, it seems that neither component of a celebrity's image is related to a change in attitude. Rather, it is the perceived *expertness* of the celebrity vis a vis the cause that carries weight with an audience. Simply put, Magic Johnson was not seen as an expert on the topic of AIDS. Consequently, his message failed to register with audiences. While Magic Johnson's motives were noble, the results of his efforts would appear to have been something less than he and others promoting the cause of AIDS would have hoped for.

50 The O.J. Simpson Verdict

On October 3, 1995, an estimated 80% of Americans listened to the verdict in the case of football superstar O. J. Simpson charged with a double-murder. The predominantly African American jury brought in a "not guilty" verdict in a case where the defense team "played the race card". A national Gallup poll taken immediately after the verdict was announced showed that among White Americans 62% disagreed with the jury's decision while 27% agreed. The remaining 11% were either undecided or declined to answer. The same poll also showed that 77% of Whites felt that the trial had hurt race relations while 53% of African Americans shared that belief.

Did the trial and verdict actually damage relations between Whites and African Americans or was the damage only to the reputation and image of this charming and gifted Hall of Famer? To answer this question, researchers had 208 White college students complete a racism scale at three points in time, i.e., one week before the verdict, one week after the verdict, and nine weeks later. The results presented in the Figure below (adapted from Nier, Mottola & Gaertner, 2000) show the extent of the damage.

During the trial (Time 1) the three groups who later thought the verdict should have been "guilty", "not guilty" and "undecided" did not differ in their racism scores. However, one week after the verdict (Time 2) both those who judged that a guilty verdict was called for and those who were undecided scored significantly higher on the racism scale. Those who agreed with the jury's "not guilty" verdict showed no change. Equally important, the damage inflicted on racial relationships by the verdict was not short-lived. As shown in the Figure, the increases observed in racist attitudes were still evident 9 weeks later (Time 3). The verdict not only changed the attitudes of many Whites but also, the increases in prejudicial attitudes appear to have been relatively long-lasting.

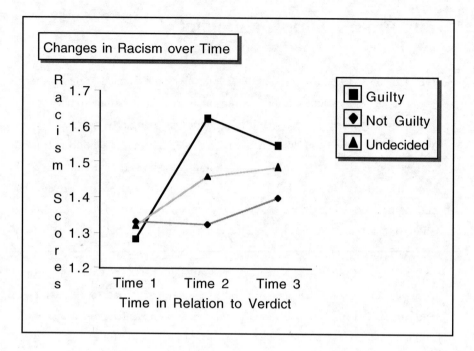

The impact of the trial also affected the behaviors of those within the Los Angeles medical community. Medical personnel were found to have dramatically increased their reporting of domestic violence situations in the aftermath of the Simpson/Goldman murders. By contrast, an earlier 1994 law mandating the reporting of such incidents to the LA Sheriff's Department had no effect on reporting whatsoever!

51 What Trading Cards Can Tell Us

Recent years have seen an explosion of interest in collecting and trading sports cards. Once a hobby for children, the market has been taken over by serious adult investors in what has become a billion dollar industry in memorabilia. Rare cards fetch prices into the thousands of dollars. Dreams of sudden wealth have sent scores of men frantically looking for their boyhood collections. Digging through the trunk in the attic without success, they come to the agonizing realization that their mother tossed them out years ago along with their collections of bottle caps and fish hooks.

Several economists have recently examined this flourishing market for its social implications. In particular, they were interested in determining if collectors/dealers showed any evidence of racial bias in their pricing of cards. Their analyses turned up clear evidence that the value of baseball cards is influenced to a large extent by the race of the athlete depicted. For example, among hitters the price of cards featuring non-White players is about 10% less than the price of White players of equal ability. Among pitchers, the cards of White players command 13% more in the marketplace than do non-Whites. Within the non-White categories, the cards of Hispanic pitchers have a higher value than the cards of Black pitchers of the same ability. However, this Hispanic - Black difference was found only among pitchers whose outstanding records allowed them to be classified as "stars". Of course, trading cards are not the only source of evidence of racial bias in baseball. Fans can also express their bias in voting for all-stars. In this case, I have something more positive to report. An examination of All-Star voting revealed that discrimination toward Black players decreased through the decades of the 70s and 80s.

As a footnote, a Mickey Mantle card is almost invariably the most valuable card in a set, often worth twice that of the second most valuable card. Undoubtedly, the most valuable card to date is one featuring Pittsburgh Pirate shortstop and Hall of Famer, Honus Wagner. His card was recently auctioned over the internet for a reported $1,100,000 US.

52   A Measure of Sport Greatness

The topic of conversation at the dinner table or at the local watering hole often turns to discussions of athletic greatness. These discussions are sometimes friendly, sometimes heated and seldom produce agreement. Not too surprising if comparisons are being made between apples and oranges, as they frequently are! For example, which was the greater performance: Bob Beamon's world record of 29' 2 1/2" in the long jump or Wilt Chamberlain's, 100-point basketball game? Is it even possible to bring some semblance of order to this debate?

Two fearless researchers, Bruce Golden and Edward Wasil have tackled the complex problem of developing a system by which outstanding sports records can be ranked from the "good" to the "truly amazing" end of the continuum. Their system, developed in 1987, is certainly not the final word on how best to compare various records. They themselves acknowledge that the importance given to some of the factors are merely their best guesses. Nonetheless, the set of considerations that they identify as important in setting some records apart from others makes for interesting speculation. So, in the interests of giving you some ammunition for future discussions (or arguments), let's have a look at what the investigators consider to be important.

To begin with, comparisons are made only among records in the same category, i.e., either single day, single season or over an athlete's entire career. One would not, for example, compare the career record of Johnny Unitas who completed touchdown passes in 47 consecutive games with Wilt Chamberlain's 100-point, single game total.

The ranking of career records is initially based on three factors individually weighted for their importance. First in importance is how well the career record has stood the test of time (weighted 500). Two considerations underlie this factor, i.e., the number of years the record has stood and the number of years it is expected to stand. The second factor is how much the record represents an improvement over the previous mark (weighted 333). Finally, a factor of other record characteristics, e.g., glamour, purity, is given a minor part in the system (weighted 167). Glamour simply reflects the fact that some records receive more attention from the media and fans than other records. Purity recognizes that an individual record achieved largely without the help of teammates, e.g., goal scoring, is more impressive than the record of another player who for example, led the league in assists.

Having considered the system itself, it becomes even more interesting to see the results of its application to single season and career records. The Figure below shows that two records overshadow all others. The touchdown passing record of Unitas is only slightly ahead of Babe Ruth's career batting average of .690. Thereafter, other career records are well down in the rankings.

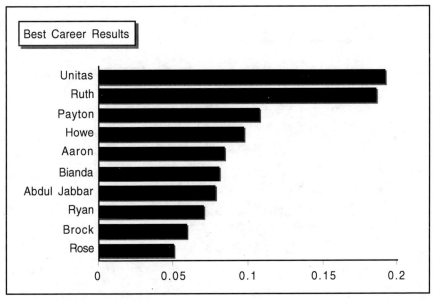

I am sure that Golden and Wasil would be among the first to agree that their model is somewhat tenuous being based on certain assumptions and a high degree of subjectivity. Still, it is a start. Perhaps more important is their identification of factors they feel contribute to a record's greatness. Of course, those of us who like to debate matters of individual achievement now have the means to argue more rationally on behalf of our own favorite candidate for greatness. Let the discussions begin!

53 How Great Thou Art

When sports aficionados with a historical bent get together around the water cooler the conversation frequently turns to matters of past greatness. Most have their favorite candidate for the greatest quarterback, the greatest goalie, the greatest pitcher, etc., of all time. However, if the debate is confined to a single performance the official records in a sport provide the means to reliably compare the quality of athletic performances from a bygone era.

One such effort involved an attempt to develop an overall measure of a batter's success at the plate that went well beyond the simple batting average. It

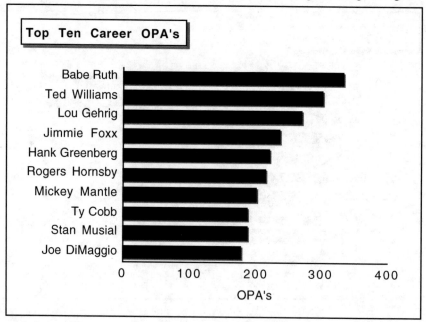

took into account additional offensive factors such as power hitting, i.e., doubles, triples and home runs, as well as the batter's success in stealing bases. The net result of all this is a measure of batting effectiveness.

The index itself is called the offensive performance average (OPA) and has been applied to the records of major league baseball going back to the early days of this century. After a great deal of number crunching, one comes up with a measure of batting effectiveness for each of baseball's legendary figures. The Figure above (adapted from Pankin, 1978) shows the top ten career OPA's up to the end of the 1975 season: (1) Babe Ruth, (2) Ted Williams, (3) Lou Gehrig, (4) Jimmie Foxx, (5) Hank Greenberg, (6) Rogers Hornsby, (7) Mickey Mantle, (8) Ty Cobb, (9) Stan Musial, (10) Joe DiMaggio.

Note that the OPA is only one of a number of possible measures assessing a batter's success at the plate. Other indices might weight the factors differently or even consider a different set of factors in assessing offensive performance at the plate. Indeed, some injustice may be done to players such as Ty Cobb who played in the "dead ball" era prior to 1920. Extra base hits that count heavily in calculating the OPA were simply not as easy to come by. In any event we have been given more fuel to fire those water cooler discussions.

54 A Record Among Records

Few people ever expected to see the amazing record-setting performances of Jesse Owens and Babe Ruth eclipsed in their lifetimes. Yet, Bob Beamon and Henry Aaron did just that. Beamon surpassed Owen's mark in the long jump and Aaron broke Ruth's career home run record. Few expected these records to fall but fall they did.

Several points should first be emphasized with reference to records. The idea of serious record keeping is a relatively new idea. The practice of recording specific features of athletic performances for present and future generations has been enthusiastically adopted by sports officials and aficionados alike. In several sports, the number of categories currently being tracked for purposes of identifying record performances has grown to absurd proportions. The fastest, the youngest, the shortest, the greatest number of...: it is fast reaching a stage where most athletes can lay claim to at least some sort of record however obscure the category. Moreover, many records are set as the result of extreme good fortune as well as athletic skill. On the other hand, bad luck can also dash one's hopes of a place in the record books. A gifted pitcher drafted by a perennial, cellar-dwelling club has little or no hope of setting league records for season or career wins.

With so many records on the books one might ask if any are truly exceptional, that is, a record among records. Obviously, one or more athletes own every record. The question being asked however, is whether any single performance is so far above the average for the category that it defies the probabilities. For example, a batter hitting 99 home runs next season would not only astound the sportsworld but also, the mathematical community. If instead, he hit 80 home runs the sportsworld might still be astounded whereas mathematicians would show little interest and likely return to solving differential equations.

Do such records exist? In baseball at least, the answer is "yes", just one. In 1941 the New York Yankee's Joe Dimaggio hit successfully in 56 consecutive games. This extraordinary achievement far surpasses the mark of 44 games held jointly by Wee Willie Keeler and Pete Rose. Just how extraordinary is Dimaggio's record? Based on the calculations of Nobel Laureate Ed Purcell, Dimaggio's record of 56 games is off the curve. Specifically, it is so many standard deviations above the historical average of such streaks that neither our grandchildren nor their grandchildren can ever expect to see the feat equalled. The remaining baseball records, while impressive, fall within the range of what would be expected by chance alone. That is, "...nothing ever happened in baseball above and beyond the frequency predicted from coin-tossing models" (Gould, 1991, p. 466). Only Joltin' Joe has the distinction of a record record, the streak of streaks!

55 Pros and Cons

What do we really know about the professional sports stars whose achievements are celebrated daily on television and in the press? Generally speaking, are they the sorts of people we want our children to respect and adopt as personal heroes? Should we be concerned with what they are like in real life? It seems reasonable to ask these questions when we look back over events of the past few years. We have seen high profile athletes involved in everything from illegal drug use and tax fraud to rape and murder. Perhaps, we are looking at only a few bad apples! I wish it were so. It appears that the number of bad apples in the barrel is greater than any of us might have guessed. So many in fact that we would be wise to look behind the headlines before placing professional athletes on a pedestal to be admired by aspiring youngsters.

A 1998 book entitled: *Pros and cons: The criminals who play in the NFL* contains some surprising findings. Based on a sample of 509 players from the 1996-'97 season, the authors found fully **21%** had been charged with a serious crime. Keep in mind that many of these men were arrested more than once. In fact, those players with a criminal record had an average of **2.4** arrests. These then are men charged with major crimes. While we may admire their achievements on the gridiron, should we hold them up as role models for our children?

Another troubling aspect of professional sports that has implications for hero choice is the number of out-of-wedlock children fathered by athletes. A story appearing in *Sports Illustrated* reveals the extent of the problem in the National Basketball Association. While firm statistics are not available, interviews with NBA insiders indicate numbers the authors describe as "staggering". A league agent is quoted as saying "... there might be more kids out of wedlock than there are players in the NBA" (Wahl & Wertheim, 1998, p. 64). A former player, agent and broadcaster estimates that "... one (out-of-wedlock child) for every player is a good ballpark figure ... for every player with none, there's a guy with two or three" (Wahl & Wertheim, 1998, p. 64).

Those concerned with the influence that negative role models have on those who admire them might take some measure of comfort from a media study. Asked about sports figures they used as personal role models, most fans emphasized a distinction between their admiration and adopting the behavior and/or ideals represented by that figure. In fact, "... very few admitted to copying any athlete in any respect except the physical accomplishment of the sports (as in emulating a golf swing)" (Eastman & Riggs, 1994, p. 262). To put an optimistic spin on the question, perhaps villainous individuals do little more than attract attention to their scandalous behavior.

There are many good men on the rosters of our major sports who conduct themselves in an honorable fashion in all aspects of their day to day lives. Many of these athletes would qualify as bonafide heroes. However, the actions of other pro athletes have made them unfit for hero status. They simply fall short of what should be expected of those in the spotlight.

Summary
The chapters in this section were organized around the central theme of outstanding performers who have been held out as heroes to the public. We touched upon the public's attitudes toward top-flight athletes and in turn, their influence in shaping our attitudes and behaviors. Also, some answers to our deep-seated need to know who among the stars in a sport shone the brightest was at least partially satisfied in several of the chapters. A concluding chapter sent a message to parents that professional stars may not be all they seem. A background check may be in order before they are placed before our children as heroes to be admired and emulated.

IX. The Sporting Environment

Introduction

With so much of our concern focussed on how to maximize the performance of athletes, it is easy to overlook the environmental circumstances in which their performances take place. Environmental features also affect the enjoyment that spectators can derive from watching an event. Indeed, owners of franchises have in most cases spared no expense in seeing to the comfort and needs of those who pay the bills and who ultimately determine the success or failure of the enterprise.

We can all remember an athletic contest whose outcome was dramatically affected by the weather. For example, professional golf tournaments are sometimes plagued by strong winds. Historically at least, Texans have surged to the top of the leader board on such occasions. Golfers learning the skills of their craft in Texas learn also to play the wind, a major feature of Texas weather systems.

Football games have similarly been played in the midst of snowstorms and bitterly cold temperatures. My favorite is the Fog Bowl played in Exhibition Stadium in 1962. At stake was the Grey Cup, emblematic of Canadian football supremacy. A dense fog rolled in shortly after the game began and it steadily got thicker. Players running onto the field disappeared from sight. Apart from the players and perhaps the officials, few people had any idea what was happening on the field. The fog thickened and the game was eventually called off. The final 10 minutes were played on the following day.

The state of the playing surface is a further factor that in some cases decides the outcome of a competition. A sloppy race course favors the "mudders". Players used to artificial turf may initially experience difficulties adjusting to natural grass. We will see in an upcoming chapter both the advantages to players of an artificial surface as well as the downside. In sum, Astro turf and aspects of the weather make up the sample of environmental topics discussed on the pages ahead. A concluding chapter in this section evaluates the success of various tactics intended to reduce the littering behavior of spectators.

56 Weather and Baseball

This chapter relies exclusively on the work of Dr. Robert K. Adair who from 1987 to 1989 held an appointment as "Physicist to the National League". His engaging 1990 paperback entitled: *The physics of baseball* offers a fascinating array of findings dealing with everything from the dynamics of a ball in flight, to the physics of pitching and batting, to the properties of various types of bats. Most of the technical stuff, formulae, calculations, etc. is conveniently tucked away at the end of each chapter leaving those of us with only a smattering of physics free to read merrily on oblivious to the underlying calculations.

Few people would be surprised to learn that the performance of baseball players and other athletes can be affected by the weather. Gusty winds make it especially difficult for outfielders to catch the high fly ball. At the same time, pitchers may lose some of their control when the temperature hovers around 95 degrees Fahrenheit. As for the performance of batters, fairly precise estimates have been made of the influence of weather factors on the flight of a well-hit pitch.

To begin with, consider the influence of the wind on the distance a ball travels when it is hit into a 10 mph headwind or alternately, a 10 mph wind blowing from the plate toward center field. Thus for example, a ball that leaves the bat at the optimum angle of 35 degrees above the horizontal at 90 mph would travel about 315 feet while one hit with a velocity of 120 mph would land about 455 feet from home plate.[5] Now note the influence of a 10 mph wind. A 400 foot drive with a following wind will land 430 feet from home base while the same 400 foot drive hit into a 10 mph headwind will drop 370 feet from home plate. What would have been a home run on a calm day is at best, a double

---

[5] an initial backspin of 2,000 rpm was assumed for these calculations.

with a breeze blowing in from center field.

Altitude is a further factor affecting the performance of batters. Home run hitters toying with the center field fence at sea level will find the same hit clears the fence with ease in cities that are well above sea level. For example, the 400-ft. drive hit in Yankee Stadium (close to sea level) will fly an additional 5 feet in Milwaukee and 6 feet in Kansas City. But these advantages to hitters pale by comparison with that provided members of Colorado's National League franchise, the Colorado Rockies. The 400-ft drive in Yankee Stadium now carries a further 40 feet! The rarefied atmosphere in the mile high city of Denver makes it a batter's paradise. In the case of long-ball hitters, being traded to the Rockies may be a blessing in disguise. Finally, Denver pitchers with a good fastball will find it a little faster. However, their curveball will not curve quite as much as it would at sea level.

Other factors can similarly affect the trajectory of the 400-ft home run. A difference of 20 feet can be expected between the distance the ball will fly on a cold day in Milwaukee (45 degrees F) and a hot afternoon in Atlanta (95 degrees F). In addition to temperature, barometric pressure similarly affects the distance a ball will travel. For each one-inch reduction in air pressure, the ball can be expected to sail a further 6 feet. Even the humidity can add extra distance. Water vapor being slightly lighter than air, very humid conditions can also add a little something extra to the long ball hit to center field. To summarize, a hot, humid day in Denver with a breeze blowing out to center field comes close to a slugger's idea of heaven.

57 Hot Players, Hot Tempers

When temperatures rise, so too do tempers. Since the riot-torn decade of the 1960s when ghetto riots flared in the inner cities of the US, the press and more recently social scientists, have established that a connection exists between high temperatures and aggression. What the press came to call the "long, hot summer hypothesis" has been found to be basically true and goes a considerable ways toward accounting for a variety of violent anti-social acts. When temperatures soar to the region of 100 F (38 Celsius) and above, police records in Texas show a corresponding rise in homicides, assaults and rape. As interesting as these studies are, many of us might not be ready at this point to accept the implication that athletes too get hot under the collar in competitions played under extremely hot conditions. Luckily, a baseball study makes it easier for the doubters among us to accept the proposition.

First off, the problem for a team of Texas researchers was to find an action in baseball that can both be measured and satisfies the requirements for a definition of aggression. They settled on the frequency with which batters at the plate are hit by pitched balls, thus filling the bill on both counts. This particular statistic was tallied from the records of a major Texas league for all games played over three seasons. Next, the temperatures at game time were found in the records of the US national weather office. Sure enough, the number of batters hit in games was found to steadily increase as temperatures rose to oppressive levels.

Rather than impugning the motives of Texas pitchers, you might be tempted instead to suggest that the increase in hits was the result of wild pitches and/or sweaty palms. Nice try! Actually, the researchers considered this explanation but were able to rule out this possibility by means of some nifty statistical gymnastics. As a result, we are left with a conclusion that the general irritation and discomfort experienced by athletes performing under extremely hot conditions can lead to interpersonal aggression.

58 Playing Under the Dome

Recent decades have seen a number of traditionally outdoor sports move indoors. Mammoth domed stadia now house sports such as baseball and football. From the point of view of the spectators, the game can be enjoyed in the comfort of a climate controlled environment, the weather being a concern only in travelling to and from the stadium.

For the athletes, domed stadia have introduced at least two important changes to their sport. First, by maintaining constant, "ideal" conditions under the dome, the vagaries of weather, e.g., wind, rain, cold, have been removed as tactical considerations from the game. However, a second important change to the game arises from the homogeneous environment provided under the dome. Players must contend with and adapt to noise levels that are considerably higher than those experienced in outdoor stadia. Sound specialists tell us that noise levels in some domed stadia often exceed 92 decibels, a level that is perceived to be twice as loud as that experienced in open-air stadia (incidentally, you might recall that in Chapter 11 high school cheerleaders peaked at 102 on the decibel scale!).

As for performance, some evidence suggests that baseball players make more fielding errors in domed stadia. Presumably, communication between players is more difficult and the auditory cues (e.g., the crack of the bat) that players use to guide their actions are often masked by crowd noise. The negative impact of noise on baseball skills can also be seen from a different perspective. Over an eight year period that involved 35,000 major league games, teams playing their home games in domed stadia won 10.5% more games at home than on the road. By contrast, teams playing home games in open-air stadia won 7.2% of their games. This shrinkage in the home field advantage represents about three fewer home games per season being won by each open-air team.

The extremely loud noise levels produced in a domed stadium can also affect the quality of play of football teams. When a comparison was made between NFL teams playing in domed versus open-air stadia, the size of the home field advantage was again greater for teams playing under the dome. A corresponding difference in the size of the home field advantage was also found in the records of teams playing in open-air stadia who subsequently acquired domed facilities. In practical terms, this difference translates into 1 1/2 to 2 points per game. One has only to look at the results of recent games to appreciate the importance of two points in changing the final outcome of numerous games.

59 Putting Sports on a Firm Footing

Anytime that sports officials consider the introduction of a technological change, we can expect their actions will stir up a flurry of controversy. Traditionalists will see any innovation as changing the basic nature of their sport and find the prospect of change not at all to their liking. Others are quick to throw their support behind changes that they see will improve athletic performance, safety, or enhance the entertainment value of the sport. The result is that some technological changes find immediate acceptance, others are introduced only gradually, while others are rejected outright.

Several major televised sports, e.g., football, baseball, ice hockey, have already seen heated controversy over the use of instant replays being made available to game officials. Other debates have focussed on the introduction of technological improvements in playing equipment. These have included aluminum bats, long-handled putters, thumbless boxing gloves and helmets/visors for hockey players. Perhaps, the most sweeping changes to sports in recent years have come with the introduction of artificial playing surfaces.

For the most part Astroturf has been generally accepted by sports fans. While some debate lingers, much of it centers on questions of its effects on the athlete's performance during a game. Does the improved footing make any difference and, if so, which part of the game benefits? In the case of baseball, we have some answers.

The performance of players in major league ballparks that had artificial turf was compared to performances in ballparks with natural grass. Over a five year period, the ballplayers were found to have a higher percentage of extra base hits and stolen bases and fewer fielding errors on the artificial surface. At the same time, there was no apparent improvement in batting averages or home runs.

Of course, there is a darker, more serious side to the debate over playing surfaces. Especially troubling is the prospect of an increase in the frequency and severity of injuries to athletes. Indeed, over a decade of research by investigators in sports medicine has confirmed that there is a medical downside to artificial turf. Some of the nastier injuries occur in football and include debilitating damage to knees and ankles. In the case of artificial turf, it appears that we don't get something for nothing. There is a price to pay, a price paid by the athletes.

60 Litterbugs and Litterbags

If you have ever remained in your seat to avoid the rush after a baseball or football game, then our impressions of our immediate surroundings are apt to be quite similar. There is litter everywhere, in some places almost ankle deep. Gum wrappers, half-eaten fries, paper cups, programs and God knows what else are strewn in the aisles and under the seats waiting for the clean-up crew. In facilities that schedule entertainment and sports events during most nights of the week, the costs of cleaning up trash can represent a sizable expenditure. If spectators could somehow be persuaded to deposit their trash in the receptacles that are provided, impressive savings could be realized. Such was the challenge undertaken by researchers at Pennsylvania State University.

Attempts were made to control littering at two consecutive Penn State football games using a variety of tactics. Some sections of the stadium were left "untreated" and used as a basis for comparisons of total litter weight with other, "treated" sections. The tactics ranged from simply handing out litter bags to providing litter bags with a label offering spectators $1.00 if the number on their bag was drawn after the game. Another version stressed good citizenship reminding spectators that "You will be a model for other people". My favorite was a negative prompting tactic intended to raise fears of social rejection, i.e., "Don't be a litterbug. Others will disapprove of your littering. Litter can hurt". Which tactic was most successful?

All four tactics were equally successful in reducing the amount of littering. When the trash was swept up from the untreated and treated (litterbag) sections and weighed, there was a whopping 45% reduction in the amount of litter discarded in the treated sections. The savings to a university or other sports facility are considerable when one considers that each clean-up at Penn State's Beaver Stadium occupies a crew of 24 workers for 6 hours. There may however, be a further ongoing environmental bonus if many of those who responsibly deposit their litter in the receptacles continue to show a concern for the environment in the weeks that follow.

Summary

In this section we have touched briefly on the role of environmental factors in affecting athletic performance as well as the emotional state of athletes. The development of artificially created environments and playing surfaces were shown to be good news for some, bad news for others. A nifty experiment conducted with college football fans showed that those with a disregard for a sporting environment can be influenced to adopt socially responsible behaviors.

A postscript

The chapter "missing" from this environmental section is one involving one of my favorite sports, golf. Have you ever wondered as I do just how much of the United States is made up of golf courses? If all the courses were laid out side by side, how large an area would they cover? Could the area be as large as a small state such as Delaware, or larger? I am also led to wonder about the depletion of a diminishing natural resource, water, already in critically short supply in some parts of the nation. Lastly, I wonder how many mega-tons of fertilizers and pesticides are dumped on the nation's courses each year to maintain their perfect, weed-free fairways and greens? Alas, I have not come across such an accounting but it would be a worthy addition to this section.

X. Risks, Health and Sports

Introduction

People are generally aware and accepting of moderate levels of risk in their day to day activities. Of course, individuals differ greatly in the levels of risk they find acceptable. Some take excessive precautions and avoid situations and practices that pose a threat to their safety and well-being. More than that, many of these people actively take steps to further reduce specific risks in their lives by using seat belts, giving up smoking and/or embarking on an exercise regimen. By contrast, others deliberately seek out situations that expose them to the possibility of harm. Whether people knowingly live on an earthquake fault or flood plain, or choose to take up hang gliding or auto racing, they are running risks that most of us would prefer to avoid.

Statistics that allow for relative comparisons of the safety of various risky sports are difficult to come by. The job of comparing sports in this regard is further complicated by the fact that some sports produce fatalities and relatively few injuries, e.g., sky diving, whereas in others, fatalities are rare but injuries are commonplace, e.g., football. Moreover, a number of sports produce injuries or long term debilitating effects that go almost unrecognized. In this section, we will see examples of sports in which the dangers are not by any means obvious, even to the athletes themselves. For many sports, steps could be taken to reduce the risks to the future health of its participants; for the boxing fraternity, there are no easy solutions in sight.

61 Exercise, Hostility and Life Expectancy

Most people are aware of at least some of the health factors that can add months, if not years, to their lives. One would think that people would see it as in their best interests to take advantage of what is known about health risks to increase their own life expectancies. Sadly, for many people such an assumption is unwarranted. They do little to reduce the stress in their lives, continue smoking, remain obese and, ignore early symptoms of life-shortening illnesses. Others actively take steps to improve the quality of their lives as well as extend their life span. With a view to reducing their vulnerability to risk factors, many people have turned to sports and/or exercise, hoping to realize overall health benefits and thereby, an increase in life expectancy. Certainly, an active rather than a sedentary life style is beneficial but is longevity necessarily increased?

It has long been recognized that people's life expectancy has been increased through our ability to ward off and/or treat infectious diseases. Many individuals have further recognized the importance of a well-balanced and nutritious diet in extending their life span. Those who are successful in quitting smoking or getting their weight down to an acceptable level can also substantially increase their longevity. It must be said though that the case for exercise has been somewhat controversial. However, studies carried out in recent years appear to make a convincing case for physical exercise being associated with a greater life expectancy.

An example of such a study was reported in the *New England Journal of Medicine* and involved the tracking of 16,936 men. These were men who had attended Harvard College sometime between 1916 and 1950. A total of 1,413 (8%) of the alumni had died when the follow up was carried out. The causes of death were: cardiovascular disease (45%), cancer (32%), other natural causes (13%) and trauma (10%). It is worth noting that in addition to investigating the role of physical activity on longevity, the researchers also examined the effects of hypertension, smoking and obesity.

As regards exercise, a single overall measure of the energy typically used in a number of activities (e.g., walking, climbing stairs, sports participation) was calculated for each of the 1,413 men who had died. The results were straightforward. As shown in the Figure below (adapted from Paffenbarger et al., 1986), there was a steady decline in the death rates as the levels of exercise by these men increased. However, there are apparently limits to the benefits of exercise. At very high levels of exercise, there was instead, a slight upturn in the death rates.

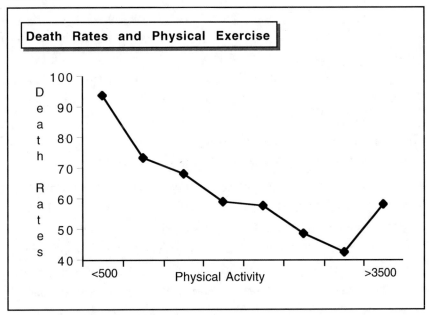

The results show a considerable advantage to being involved in some form of vigorous exercise on a regular basis. The trend is clear. Starting with those Harvard alumni who got little in the way of exercise (<500 kcal.), we see a death rate of 93.7 per 10,000 man years. Thereafter, the mortality rate steadily declines with increasing involvement in physical exercise. Only when 3,500 kcals of energy are expended do we see a slight upturn in the death rate.

The study also supported common beliefs regarding the life-shortening potential of other risk factors. Death rates were considerably higher among men who were cigarette smokers, hypertensive (e.g., high blood pressure) and among those who had gained excessive weight since their college days.

How was the amount of exercise taken by their subjects calculated? It was assessed in several ways that included the number of miles they typically walked, the number of stairs they climbed, the type of sports they were involved in and the time devoted weekly to sports participation. However, the overall effects of exercise is probably best seen in a measure of physical activity (kilocalories) that combined all of the above measures.

Another way to approach the question of exercise and longevity is to look specifically at people's level of participation in sports. Again, Harvard men provided the basic data of a study. A total of 2,190 men born between 1860 and 1889 were classified as either major athletes, minor athletes or non-athletes. Major athletes were men who had lettered in major varsity sports, e.g., football, rowing, track. Minor athletes included those who failed to win a letter and others who were involved in Harvard's minor sports program, e.g., cricket, golf, swimming. Non-athletes either had no records of participation or participation only in their freshman year. The results provide an interesting slant on the relationship between levels of physical exercise and life expectancy. It was the category of minor athletes that lived longest. They clearly outlived both their extremely active and relatively inactive classmates. At the same time, the longevity of major athletes and non-athletes did not differ. It would appear that efforts to extend one's life span are most likely to be successful when they involve participation in moderately strenuous and demanding activities. Excessive exertion in highly demanding sports/activities may be ineffective in extending one's life span. That is, more is not always better.

In concluding this section on longevity, a less commonly recognized risk factor deserves mention. In a number of rivalrous sports, e.g., soccer, fans and athletes alike harbor considerable hostility toward opposing teams and their supporters. When that hostility becomes an enduring feature of one's personality on a day to day basis, it poses a major health risk with life-shortening implications.The Figure below (adapted from Barefoot et al., 1983) shows the death rates for two groups of physicians. As medical students, the subjects were divided on the basis of high or low scores on a standard measure of trait hostility and thereafter tracked across a 25-year period. What we see is a dramatic increase in the number of deaths among those who back in medical school were identified as hostile individuals. Easier said than done, perhaps these people can be led

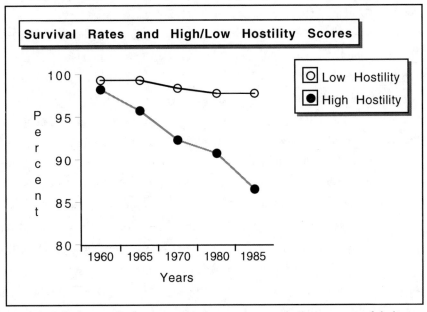

to shift their focus of attention away from anger-producing aspects of their sport to an appreciation of athletic skill, irrespective of winning or losing.

62   Do Right–handers Outlive Southpaws?

With apologies, the section to follow is likely to be unsettling for 10 to 12% of my readers. The readers I have in mind are those who are left- handed. Stanley Coren and Dianne Halpern have presented findings that suggest left-handers live an average of 8 fewer months than right-handers. This surprising conclusion is brought home for sports fans by a study that examined the records of major league baseball.

Let us look at a key piece of evidence pointing to a longer life span for right-handers. Baseball players were first classified as either right (a total of 1,472) or left-handers (N = 236). Only those who pitched and batted from the same side were included in the analyses. A difference in average life expectancy was again found just as in other studies. Additionally, it was noted that the last surviving southpaw died at age 91; the oldest right-handed player survived to 109.

A further study examined the records of British cricketers from 1864 to 1983. With bowling hand as the indicator of handedness, 2,580 men were identified as right-handed while 585 were lefties. The difference in life expectancy again favored right-handers, in this case by a little over 2 years.

The most intriguing question of all is "why". What is there about being left-handed that could possibly be life-shortening? For starters, any lefty will tell you that life presents them with more than their share of frustrations. The world has essentially been designed by right-handers for right-handers. Industrial machinery, kitchen appliances, automobiles and school desks present a continuing challenge for those whose left hand is dominant. One suggestion is that stress and the inevitable miscalculations in coping with day to day circumstances leads to life shortening accidents to left-handers. These findings on accident involvement suggest that lefties can increase their life expectancies by recognizing their susceptibility and adopting safer practices. So lefties, beware! It's a right-handed jungle out there.

Another leading explanation points to differences in physiology. It appears that women who give birth to left-handers have longer and more difficult deliveries. Equally significant, their babies weighed less at birth. A further explanation suggests that the immune systems of left-handers may be weaker than those of right-handers. These deficiencies may make left-handers less able to withstand the rigors of life, i.e., less able to survive accidents and/or ward off disease.

Left-handers should however, be reassured by the fact that the handedness research described above deals with "averages". The fact is that the distribution of life expectancies for the two groups has considerable overlap. Vast numbers of left-handers outlive their right-handed contemporaries. It is only "on average" that the two groups differ in life expectancy.

Finally, there is no reason to doubt the abilities of left-handers to excel in sports, as elsewhere. Every sport can point to one or more top flight athletes who have left their mark (e.g., Conners, Koufax, Mickelson, etc.). There is also no shortage of talented left-handers in other fields of endeavour from Alexander the Great, Queen Victoria, Charles Chaplin, Picasso to Winston Churchill. As nearly everyone is aware, the US White House has been continuously occupied by southpaws since the Kennedy administration. Even the recently elected President promises to continue the tradition of left-handed, political leadership. So, if you are left- handed, you are in very good company.

Left-handers, take heart! If Stanley Coren's findings on life expectancy have left you feeling depressed, you might find subsequent reviews of research on the topic more heartening. It seems that several researchers examining handedness and longevity in other populations have been unable to reproduce the early findings. Now, it must be said that when a researcher's results are difficult to replicate we view the original conclusion with less certainty. It must also be pointed out that presently a number of researchers are hotly debating his findings on other grounds. In any case, I would anticipate that much more will be heard from the scientific community on this topic. In the meantime be of good cheer.

63 The Silent Epidemic: Boxing's Dark Side

Sports offer participants a variety of important benefits. At a recreational level, sports offer participants an increased sense of well-being, intrinsic satisfactions from mastering new skills and an enriched social life. For the professional athlete, sports may additionally provide wealth, fame and status. Enthusiasts are quick to point out these benefits in publicizing and promoting their particular sport. Much less is said about the downside of some sports, especially those where the risk of injuries is high.

Certainly, there is an ever present risk of accidents in the home and workplace. Indeed, participants in many sports are exposed to risks that are no greater; in some sports the risks may even be less. We may for example, actually be safer on the golf course or in the bowling alley than crossing the street or driving to and from work. However, for other sports there is a darker and seldom publicized side to participation. While injuries can be sustained to all parts of the body and result in short or long-term disabilities, I want to direct your attention to one of the most serious, yet generally unrecognized type of injury, that of head trauma.

Described by experts in the field as the silent epidemic, mild head injuries can produce a number of symptoms that include memory loss, headaches, depression, attentional deficits, lowered sexual drive and an intolerance to alcohol. If we consider only head injuries occurring in sports, a mere handful of sports come to mind as contributing the lion's share of head trauma cases. Leading the way is boxing. While studies have investigated head trauma in equestrian events, football and rugby, it is boxing that has received most of the attention from researchers. After all, it is a sport that has the sanctioned and unabashed purpose of deliberately inflicting injury.

The name commonly given to boxers who have suffered the effects of repeated head trauma is "punch drunk" or to use a more scientific term, "dementia pugilistica". Included among the symptoms of this condition are an unsteady gait, speech and motor loss, and upper body tremors. Neurologists speak with one voice in answering the question of the long term effects of sustained blows to the head. The brain damage resulting from repeated concussions add up and beyond a certain point are pretty much irreversible with scientists offering only a glimmer of hope for the future. That is, unlike a broken limb, the brain does not automatically heal itself.

At the risk of oversimplification, the brain can be likened to a quivering mass of cells with a consistency not unlike that of jello. It lies protected and encased within the cavity of the skull. However, there are connections between the brain and the skull in the form of innumerable capillaries that carry the blood supply to the outer surface of the brain. Now visualize if you will, what happens when a blow is struck to the head. The hardened skull snaps back with the force of the blow. The gelatinous mass of the brain, lying loosely within the skull cavity, does not as readily follow the path taken by the skull. The result is that the connecting capillaries are torn and damaged with a severe blow. As a consequence, the blood supply essential for brain functions is reduced.

How serious are the effects of repeated blows to the head and what can it mean for the individual in the long run? Consider the case of 10 professional boxers who were examined shortly after they had been knocked out. All had suffered mild head injuries. Moreover, 8 had sustained additional neurological damage. Five had abnormal CT scans, 2 had abnormal EEG readings and another exhibited neurological abnormalities. But let me put this in even more concrete terms.

There is some evidence to suggest a link between participation in boxing and later symptoms of Alzheimer's disease. Eight former fighters underwent thorough neurological assessments; all were diagnosed with Alzheimers. However, the picture worsens. Three of the boxers also presented symptoms of Parkinson's disease. There is one further point that deserves mention. The amount of brain damage suffered by a fighter is unrelated to their skill as a boxer. Instead, the amount of damage is related to the number of fights they have had. The damaged state of their brain is the result of the sum total of all blows to the head. Whether they won most of their fights or lost most of their fights is of little consequence.

A footnote to soccer Moms and Dads

The occasional banging of heads is a recognized feature of soccer matches and practice sessions. Players also suffer blows each time they head the ball. Considering the brain damage to boxers noted above, it is not unreasonable to ask if soccer players suffer any ill effects from their participation. It appears that soccer is not without risks. When a group of Dutch amateur soccer players was compared to athletes involved in swimming and track, the performance of soccer players was found to be impaired on two intellectual tests. Fully 39% were deficient on a test of planning while 27% exhibited impaired memory. Furthermore, 27% had suffered a concussion during their amateur careers with 23% having had 2 to 5 concussions. Not surprisingly, the more concussions players had suffered, the poorer their performance on the battery of neuropsychological tests. The health implications of these findings are far reaching when one considers the worldwide popularity of the game.

Although I have tried to provide a balanced perspective on the various topics discussed in this book, it is well-nigh impossible in the case of boxing. The cold, hard neurological facts point only to increasing irreversible brain damage with each blow a boxer sustains. Fewer rounds, heavier gloves and helmets may slow the progression of brain injuries but the injuries occur nonetheless. Sport officialdom, promoters and boxing enthusiasts regularly ignore or dismiss the dark side of their sport. However, the high costs should not be lost on parents of boxing hopefuls and those planning recreational programs. It is for good reason that the American, British and Canadian Medical Associations have called for a ban on boxing.

64 Keeping your Ball on the Fairway

There are dangers lurking in the woods and tangled underbrush just a few yards off the plush, manicured fairways of the modern golf course. Besides the obvious wasps, poisonous snakes and razor sharp thorns, we can now add to the list a less obvious danger that is lying in wait for those of us with a chronic slice (or hook), namely, ticks.

Ticks are increasingly being recognized as carriers of several life-threatening diseases. In addition to a risk of Rocky Mountain Spotted fever and Lyme disease, ticks (specifically, the Lone Star tick) put us at a measurable risk for Ehrlichiosis.

When a team of medical researchers compared the memberships of two golf-oriented retirement communities in Tennessee, their results provided several insights into the ways that people can inadvertently increase their risk for these illnesses. Golf courses in the first community (A) bordered on a wildlife management reserve whereas the second nearby course (B) was situated in open farmland and was separated from the wildlife reserve by a six-lane highway.

Of the eleven cases of Ehrlichiosis that were identified, ten were in community (A) alongside the wildlife reserve. Of these, all patients were male and eight of the ten were golfers. But golfers did not stand an equal chance of being infected. It was the poorer golfers with high handicaps that were infected by tick bites. Furthermore, those who characteristically went into the bushes to retrieve their ball rather than playing a new ball were also more likely to be infected. Finally, those golfers who do not routinely use insect repellent and additionally, went into the woods in search of their ball were the highest risk of all. Perhaps, we should require manufacturers to put a warning label on golf balls: "A slice can be hazardous to your health"

65 Designated Spitters

We have all seen the television camera move in for a close up shot of a ball player only to have him spit for the benefit of the viewing audience. Most of us have also wondered about the poor fellow who has the thankless job of cleaning the dugout at the end of the game. Aesthetic considerations aside, the use of spit tobacco presents a number of serious health risks to users, notably oral cancer and periodontal disease.

Who uses spit tobacco? Among professional baseball players, 35 to 40 percent use spit tobacco and approximately one half of these men have associated lesions. Furthermore, a large scale survey of 16 California colleges showed that Native Americans (48%) and Whites (44%) were the heaviest users and Blacks (11%), the lowest. Among baseball players, 52% reported using spit tobacco in contrast to 26% among football players. Use was also greater among athletes from rural backgrounds attending colleges located in rural areas.

We might also suspect that among sports fans it would be those who are most dedicated and involved in sports who are the heavy users of tobacco products. Not so! It seems that dedicated sports fans and those with little interest in sports do not differ in their consumption of either cigarettes, smokeless tobacco or alcohol.

What do smokeless tobacco users believe about their habit? While they recognize that spit tobacco is addicting and causes cancer of the mouth, they also believe that it helps them to relax, relieves boredom, improves their mood and helps them to concentrate. Close to 15% of the college athletes also felt that spit tobacco was helpful in improving their performance.

At a social level, users did not see their habit as somehow improving their appearance or image nor did they see it as providing increased acceptance by others. At the same time, women are thought to be non-discriminating: users believe that women are just as willing to go out on dates with spit tobacco users as with non-users (is it just me or are these men delusional?).

What might motivate users to quit? They see the leading factors that might prompt them to quit to be "seeing changes in their teeth and gums" and advice from their dentist. A wife or girlfriend might also be successful in persuading them to quit. The least influential are professional players (role models).

66 Referees, Umpires and Stress

From my perspective, one of the least attractive roles in sports is that of a game official. Rarely thanked or respected except by other sport officials, they are the frequent targets for abuse from a number of quarters. But it is not just abuse from disgruntled elements that makes the job stressful. Other sources can also add to their burden.

While a great deal of effort has gone into helping athletes manage their stress, officials have until recently been largely ignored. As with many occupations, job stress is a legitimate matter of concern. The effects of stress on mental health and job performance are well documented. Equally important for a sport, stress is sometimes a cause of officials leaving their sport for less stressful pastures. What do referees and umpires have to say about the things they find stressful in their job? In the case of baseball and softball umpires, the causes of stress can be grouped into four categories.

First and foremost, they experience stress in critical games and situations where their decisions often determine the outcome of a contest. The second major source of stress is a continuing fear of physical harm. In some of our major sports there is an ever-present threat of assault by coaches, players and fans. Time pressures provide a third source of stress for game officials. The problems of juggling their officiating duties with their full time occupation and with the demands of family and friends is often difficult. Finally, the interpersonal conflicts that frequently erupt during a contest add to the stress load. These conflicts involve protests by players and coaches who don't always know the rules, as well as abusive players and hostile coaches who lack self-control.

Roughly, the same four sources of stress are cited by officials in football, soccer and volleyball. However, it remains for me to put the level of stress experienced by sport officials into perspective. Far from approaching that experienced by test pilots and brain surgeons, the levels fall in the mild range. Of course, levels will vary from one official to another and from one contest to another. Even so, mild chronic stress can eventually exact a price from all of us.

67 Warmups: A Bit of a Stretch

From the earliest days of our high school gym classes to our later participation in a variety of sports and recreational activities, we have all had the importance of a warm-up drilled into our heads. Our failure to perform a short program of stretching exercises could leave us vulnerable to injury, most likely a muscle pull. But, are we really taking a foolish risk by ignoring this time-honored advice? Apparently not!

Researchers in Australia conducted a large scale, year-long study involving over 1,500 army recruits. Two groups were formed on a random basis with one group stretching leg muscles before exercise, the other group bypassing the stretching routine. For exercise instructors everywhere, the results are likely to be surprising. The two groups of men did not differ in their injury rates, i.e., soft-tissue injuries and bone injuries. However, several other factors were found to be related to injury rates.

As you might have guessed, the initial fitness level of the recruits was clearly an important consideration with the fittest having fewer injuries over the course of their training. Age was also an important factor, the young being less susceptible to injury. A curious finding deserving of further investigation was that the rate of injury among recruits who enlisted late in the year was more than twice that of those who enlisted early in the year.

As for recommendations, the authors of this study make the reasonable suggestion that injuries are more likely to be prevented by introducing a fitness training program for those among the new recruits who are the least fit. Stretching does not appear to be the answer. Still, tradition dies hard. All that can be said at this point is that there is little evidence to support the notion that stretching will reduce injuries.

Summary

Although we have only touched on a few sports and issues of safety, the underlying message is clear. It is obviously in everyone's best interests to take a closer look at those sports and activities we plan to take up. The responsibility is especially heavy for parents and educators who typically make decisions regarding sport choices on behalf of youngsters. The difficulty they face is that of finding accurate information on the prevalence of injuries and other health risks. My best and only suggestion is to dig into the sports medicine literature. The reference librarian at most college and university libraries should be more than pleased to direct you to the relevant sources. They are nice people.

XI. Media and the Business of Sports

Introduction

It is a fact of modern life that commercial interests have become closely intertwined with a majority of sports. In North America at least, the organization of sports is such that teams and individual athletes generally require financial support if they are to compete effectively and refine their skills. Seemingly, money is needed at all levels for uniforms, the latest in equipment technology, coaches and of course, travel. Corporate sponsors, the taxpayer through government grants and fund raising campaigns provide the bulk of support for this burgeoning enterprise. All but gone are the days when local athletes formed local teams and competed regionally with the support of volunteers.

Given the pervasive presence of commercial interests in virtually all sports, it is perhaps not surprising that studies in what might be called a management-marketing tradition have sprung up in recent years. The focus of these studies has been on the impact of various factors on financial returns. We see for example in the chapters to follow that the interest is on how attendance at sporting events might be affected by player violence, race or television coverage of an event. For colleges and universities, a perennial question is how to loosen the purse strings of their grateful alumni. The chapters ahead then, include a smattering of interesting findings on a number of key questions that pertain to the financial health of several sports.

68 Sport Preferences on Television

Sports have come to occupy a major segment of daily television programming. The needs of even the most avid sports enthusiast are met by round-the-clock, all-sports channels as well as sites on the internet. Within the variety of televised sports available to viewers, what are the viewing preferences of the average sports fan?

US Audiences

The preferences of American sports fans are seen in the results of a telephone survey of over 700 adults in Indianapolis and Los Angeles. Easily the most popular sport is professional football with 34.5% of respondents indicating that it is their "most watched" sport. Professional basketball and baseball were next with 13.4% and 13.2%, respectively. Next in line were college basketball 8.9%, college football 7.5% and tennis at 5.7%. Trailing the field as the most watched sport with less than 2% were golf, auto racing, gymnastics, hockey and boxing.

A closer look at the results of the survey reveals some interesting regional and sex differences. For example, pro basketball is watched far more frequently in LA than in Indianapolis. By contrast, college basketball is King in Indianapolis but is largely ignored by residents of Los Angeles. Predominantly male audiences watch football and basketball at both the professional and college levels. However, women show considerably more interest than men in baseball and tennis.

And now a question for two cultures that share the airwaves. Do preferences in viewing change as we step North across the 49th parallel into Canada?

Canadian Audiences

The results of a national survey conducted by Canada's preeminent pollster, Reginald Bibby in 1995, provides the opportunity to make a cross-border comparison. It immediately becomes clear that Canadian viewing preferences are dramatically different from those of US audiences.

Approximately 40% of Canadian viewers watch sports programming, men more so than women. Not too surprisingly, National Hockey League telecasts top the list (31%) followed closely by figure skating (30%) and major league baseball (26%). Some distance back, we find the Canadian Football League, pro golf, auto racing and the National Football League grouped at approximately 13% each. Curling, skiing and pro tennis make a respectable showing averaging just under 10% each. Bringing up the rear with less than 5% each are the National Basketball Association, Canadian university football and professional wrestling.

Regional differences in preferences are apparent. The Canadian Football League draws considerably more interest from Westerners and, to a slightly less extent, viewers in Ontario. Interest lags in the Atlantic provinces and is all but dead in Quebec. Long a stronghold of curling, viewers from the Western provinces show the strongest interest in watching the sport followed by viewers in Atlantic Canada. Finally, figure skating has a strong following among Canadian women (42%) whereas a mere 16% of Canadian men admit watching the sport.

It is unlikely that the comparison I've made is the final word on the question of US - Canadian viewing preferences. The two polls were taken several years apart using quite different means (telephone vs questionnaires) of soliciting responses. Still, the two sets of results are so substantially different that while we might quibble about specifics, to me the overall picture is one of clear cultural differences in television viewing preferences.

69 Does Televising College Football Hurt Attendance?

The question of whether televising college football games hurts attendance was the central issue in a case that came before the United States Supreme court in 1984. Up until that time, the National Collegiate Athletic Association (NCAA) had complete control over football telecasts. They argued that their regulation of televised games was necessary in order to protect participating schools from a drop in in-stadium attendance. The courts however, rejected the arguments of the NCAA noting that there was a lack of evidence showing that television coverage led to a decline in gate attendance. As a result of the ruling, individual schools were free to negotiate contracts with cable networks. The airwaves were quickly flooded with college games.

A study that followed on the heels of the Supreme court ruling produced findings that supported the court's decision. Based upon a pre-deregulation period in which television coverage of college football had rapidly expanded, the study concluded that televising games and attendance were "complementary". That is, the overall effects of televising college games was believed to increase attendance. However, this study was not the last word on the question.

A subsequent investigation of the issue used both pre- and post-regulation data in a more detailed analysis that included 93 Division 1-A schools. To quote the researchers' conclusion "... on average, the net effect of own-team and the general level of telecasts is to reduce attendance" (Fizel & Bennett, 1989, p. 988). These findings then, support the view of the NCAA who argued that if control of telecasting passed from their hands to the individual schools attendance would suffer as a result. While this may not be the final word on the question, my reading of these and other studies causes me to lean strongly in the direction of the NCAA view. If attendance is decreased by television coverage, then several important points should be borne in mind. Football fans in television audiences are better served as a result of having a wider choice of games. At the same time however, the revenues to football programs and their institutions are obviously down. The unknown factor in all of this is whether the loss in gate receipts is offset by revenues from television contracts.

Any loss in revenues is a serious matter both for football programs and the funding of education at the colleges they represent. By one estimate, gate receipts represent over 50% of the revenues of Division 1-A football teams. Additionally, funds from athletic programs that are normally turned over to an institution's educational programs may not be forthcoming. The impact of a decline in attendance at football games then has the potential to affect the quality of education in institutions of higher learning.

70 Predicting College Team Standings

A popular feature of *Sports Illustrated*, in addition to the swim suit edition, is their annual predictions of college football. Each summer a panel of "experts" provide readers with their ranking of the top 25 teams for the upcoming season of play. Just how expert are these experts? When *Sports Illustrated* predicted the final ranking of college football teams for an upcoming season of play, the results were not impressive. In only 4 of 10 conferences was there any relationship between the predictions of *Sports Illustrated* and final standings.

Other groups of experts have been assembled to make pre-season predictions for football and basketball. Writers and sportscasters make up a panel for the Associated Press (AP) wire service while coaches provide rankings for the United Press International (UPI). The accuracy of the AP and UPI football predictions were tested for 5 seasons of play. In only 2 of the 5 years were the AP and UPI forecasts related to end of season rankings. When we look at the success of AP and UPI forecasts for basketball, the results are if anything, worse. Both wire services were accurate in 1 season with the UPI also accurate in a second, again, over 5 seasons of play. For the remaining season, the forecasts were no better than what would be expected by chance.

Surprising isn't it that these carefully selected blue ribbon panels enjoy so little success in forecasting the performances of football and basketball teams. It is hard to imagine anyone better qualified to make such judgments. Writers and sportscasters are close to the game, experienced and knowledgeable, coaches even more so! If there is a lesson in all of this it must be that forecasts of this sort are wrong more often than they are right. Sure, they may be entertaining to read but when they promise a glimpse into the future it is mostly illusion.

71 Race and Attendance

Events occurring almost daily remind us that racism remains a pervasive theme in society. Most of us also recognize that sports organizations have historically discriminated against minority group athletes by way of lower salaries and practices that block their advancement to positions of authority. Not surprisingly, sports fans are also guilty of discrimination, albeit in less obvious ways.

One of the subtle ways that fans show their disdain for a minority group is seen in their decisions to attend or not attend a sports event featuring a preponderance of minority group athletes. Economists have examined this question by first comparing the racial mix of National Basketball Association teams with the racial composition of the NBA franchise cities in which they perform. They found that the closer the racial match between teams and the cities they represent, the greater the attendance. Thus, a predominantly White team playing in a predominantly Black area will not do well at the box office. Alternately, a Black team does not fare well in a community where a majority of the fans are White. The results of these studies are even more specific. It is the racial composition of the starters on the team rosters that most strongly influence fan attendance in the NBA. They are after all, the most visible representatives of their team.

Something very similar happens in baseball. Fewer fans attend National League games pitched by Blacks than those pitched by Whites. This drop in attendance was found to occur despite the fact that Black pitchers had better pitching records than Whites. More specifically, it appears that attendance drops only when the starting pitcher for the home team is non-White. The race of the visiting team's pitcher does not influence attendance.

Additionally, it appears that sports organizations are not color blind when it comes to recruiting players. In drafting players, NBA teams are ever-mindful of the racial composition of the fans in their catchment area. They too seem to recognize the importance to the bottom line of a team mirroring its fans and recruit accordingly.

The racial composition of basketball and baseball teams appears related to the number of fans pushing through the turnstiles. However, the question of racial diversity on teams and team performance has only recently been clarified. Timmerman used nearly a half century of NBA and MLB records of approximately 8,000 basketball and 20,000 baseball players in examining the possible influence of racial diversity on team performance, i.e., winning percentage. Simply put, predominantly all-White or all-Black basketball teams did better in the win-loss column than teams with a more balanced racial mix. By contrast, the extent of racial diversity on baseball teams bore no relationship to their performance on the diamond. The explanation lies with the fact that unlike baseball, basketball is a highly interdependent sport in which smooth and coordinated interactions among a team's players are essential for success on the court.

72 Win One for the Giver

One of the most cherished beliefs of college administrators is the notion that winning teams generate increased revenues from ever-so-proud alumni. Researchers in Notre Dame's Department of Marketing conducted an extensive study of the question in 1984. Their study used data provided by 99 universities that participated in major athletic programs (NCAA Division 1A). Several measures of benefactor giving were examined over the decade of the 70's in relation to the win/loss records of each institution in football and basketball.

The results were entirely in agreement with the findings of earlier studies on the question. There was simply no relationship between winning and alumni giving. If there was a surprise to be found in the results it was evidence of a slight (nonsignificant) tendency indicating that, if anything, "... winning athletic teams seem to induce a smaller amount of monetary contributions!" (Gaski & Etzel, 1984, p. 31). Perhaps, the alumni feel that winning is its own reward.

Perhaps, this is not the entire story. Possibly, alumni who strongly identify with their college teams or former athletes would be more likely to open up their wallets. The first possibility, that alumni who had strong ties to the basketball and football teams during their college days would be especially generous, was tested in a recent study. Somewhat surprisingly, there were no relationships between alumni's level of identification and donations to either the general fund of the university or the athletic department. Moreover, those who had played for the university's basketball or football teams similarly showed no greater inclination to donate than other alumni. At this juncture, university coffers do not appear to be a beneficiary of athletic success.

73   Snippets from the Indy 500

With the exception of WW II, every year since 1911 the month of May has featured the Indianapolis 500 car race from the "brickyard" in the Indianapolis suburb of Speedway, Indiana. The annual spectacle attracts daily crowds in excess of 100,000 during the time trials leading up to the actual race on Memorial Day. Race day itself attracts an estimated 400,000 spectators in addition to a vast international television audience.

Death is a constant presence at the track and has prompted one critic to paraphrase the starter's instructions to drivers: "Gentlemen, start your coffins!". In contrast to European road courses, the Indy track was designed for an earlier era and slower speeds. It is ringed with unforgiving concrete walls leaving few avenues of escape for drivers in trouble. Deaths at Indianapolis have averaged slightly more than one per year throughout the history of the event. Beyond that, one quarter of all drivers who have raced at Indy have been killed elsewhere in race cars.

What do we know about the psychological profile of these drivers? Far from being daft, suicidal or both, they are emotionally stable individuals with nerves of steel fully able to maintain control and remain calm in life-threatening situations. They also tend to be strongly competitive, assertive and self-sufficient, a combination of traits that makes them exceedingly difficult to live with. Socially, they are somewhat introverted and hold strong conservative values, e.g., hard work, honesty, etc. Perhaps, their single most distinguishing characteristic is an IQ that is well above average. When asked what occupation they would prefer if they couldn't race cars, a majority say "fighter pilot".

The time trials are almost as important to the drivers as the race itself. There are tactical as well as financial incentives for qualifying for the front row positions. Driving in heavy traffic and trying to move up through the field during the early laps of the race greatly increases the chances of being involved in an accident. In a very real sense, the safest place for a driver to be during the early stages is out front

Who will win this year's classic? History tells us that we can look to the front of the starting lineup for the eventual winner. Over the years, 45% of winning drivers started from the front row. Fully 72% of winning drivers emerged from the first three rows, i.e., the top nine qualifiers in the 33 car field.

74 Sex Sells, How about Violence?

Hollywood and the television industry have always assumed that violence, like sex, is "good box office". The two themes are closely linked in the public mind and both ingredients can be big box office draws. Some years ago I listened to the comments of a US television network executive participating in an international symposium on the media. Faced with strong public criticism at the time, he was pleased to announce that the upcoming Fall schedule would contain fewer violent programs and more "jiggle shows". The speaker apparently believed that any loss in network revenues resulting from a reduction in violent content would be offset by an increase in the returns from sexually titillating themes.

I have no quarrel with the proposition that sex in media productions is an attraction for most people nor, for that matter, with making non-violent erotica available to adult audiences. It is however, a major miscalculation to equate the drawing power of violence with that of sex. While violence is clearly an attraction for some elements in society, it does not follow that it is an attraction for people in general. In fact, television studies in the US, Canada and Finland have failed to support the common assumption that audiences generally find entertainment value in violent scenes. This conclusion applies equally to the sports box office.

Several studies in ice hockey have looked at the relationship between attendance figures and levels of player violence during different seasons of play. In the case of junior hockey, it was found that attendance at the next home game following each team's two most violent games did not differ from attendance following their two most peaceable games. However, the picture is muddied by the results of studies of attendance in the National Hockey League (NHL). For example, a 1993 investigation found that as player violence (total penalty minutes) increased, so too did attendance. But, there was an interesting twist when only the more extreme forms of violence were considered, i.e., major and misconduct penalties. An increase in attendance went hand in hand with increased player violence only in American franchise cities. A leading explanation would allow that the sport was vigorously marketed on its violent content through the expansion years.

It is clear that there is a narrow market for violence among certain individuals, particularly those who are themselves aggressive. It is further apparent that among fans of contact sports, there are those who dislike its violent aspects and others who are attracted by the prospect of player fights. With this in mind, it is interesting to speculate on what lies behind the finding that gate receipts are unrelated to game violence in junior hockey. My own guess is that any increase in the number of fans attending in hopes of seeing fights is offset by roughly equal numbers of spectators who deplore violence and who resolve not to attend the next home game following a fight-filled match. Overall then, the net effect is minimal. While violence is generally not a strong attraction for most people, it has nonetheless been tailored to meet the need for violent fare of a segment of a sport's following, e.g., the NHL.

75 Sex, Violence and Videogames

Videogames represent a $6 billion a year US industry. A booming videogame technology has attracted an enormous following among young people. At the same time, their popularity has been accompanied by controversy regarding the effects of games on players. The focus of that concern is on the violent content. By one estimate, 71% of videogames contain anti-social or violent themes.

Among the top sellers is *Mortal Combat*, a game that is not for the faint of heart. Characters on the screen are killed by ripping out their hearts, electrocution or decapitation, with the added spectacle of a partially severed, quivering spinal cord. Should this prove too tame, the player can opt for advanced graphics that include gushing blood. Even so, videogames have their supporters.

Some have contended that games provide players with a sense of control, mastery and accomplishment. Others attribute an improvement in fine motor skills and an increase in self-esteem to video play. Former President Ronald Reagan expressed the view that video practice would expand the pool of skilled future Top Guns, that is fighter pilots, available for service in the US Air Force.

A surprising number of studies has examined the social effects of video games. They suggest that the effects on players are far from benign. For example, children interact more aggressively if they have earlier played a videogame. Indeed, the more violent the game, the greater the interpersonal aggression that results. Just as with television programming, the viewing of violent content appears to increase the hostility of viewers. In addition to increased hostility, players experience increases in anxiety and cardiovascular activity, for example heart rate and blood pressure. Finally, there is a sharp decrease in altruism or helping behavior on the part of players.

The viewing of violent portrayals in video games differs in at least one important respect from violence on television or that witnessed by sports fans in the stands. Videogame players are able to exert **control** over the course of the game, setting the pace and/or intensity of events on the screen. The fact that players can exert control over events raises the possibility that the effects of viewing violence in this form may be somewhat weaker than passively viewing it on television or in sports audiences. Researchers at Utrecht University (The Netherlands) have shown that simply giving players a remote control as they watched a *Rambo* film clip resulted in fewer negative mood reactions than those not equipped with a remote. They suggest that the negative effects of viewing (sports) violence on television or as spectators may, as a result of this element of control, be somewhat reduced in the case of video games.

The presence of sexual themes in video games and of course, on television have also raised concerns in some quarters. Special interest groups are actively campaigning in many communities to ban or restrict access to X-rated or erotic materials, with the expectation that interpersonal violence in society will somehow be reduced. However, they are on the wrong track. Erotic media fare, devoid of violent themes or content, does not cause an increase in aggression. In fact, mild forms of erotica such as magazine centerfolds can instead, lead to a reduction in viewer aggression. Rather than banning naughty pictures, the efforts of those special interest groups are more likely to meet with success if redirected toward the television and videogame industries whose products so frequently contain excessively violent themes.

Summary

One of the more attractive features of research in the sports-marketing tradition is the availability of valid measures of financial success/failure. The extent of alumni giving expressed as dollars presented a convincing case for the results we saw. Almost as convincing is the use of attendance figures to represent the attraction of fans to an event (bear in mind that promoters occasionally "paper the house"). In this case researchers have provided solid evidence in place of homespun theories that for years have swirled around questions of how television coverage, player violence and racial balance/imbalance might affect the box office. This is not to say that a single study or even a series of studies are the final word on an issue. Rather, they take us a step closer to the truth of a matter than we've previously been. Future studies may yet reveal subtleties or even conflicting results. However, to date they provide the best insights available.

XII. The Face of Violence

Introduction

Few segments in today's society are free from the threat of violence. It occurs with disheartening regularity on the streets, in homes, schools, the workplace and in sports. The sportsworld has witnessed aggression at all levels, between athletes, among spectators, and on rare occasions, between athletes and spectators.

In setting the stage for this chapter, I first want to highlight a distinction for those interested in the topic of controlling aggression in sport. Not everyone recognizes that sports aggression is controlled by two overlapping authorities. Fans of some major sports, e.g., football, baseball, basketball, hockey, who become embroiled in fights or other disturbances are summarily dealt with by the local police and court system. A few feet away on the playing surface, virtually the same sorts of interpersonal aggression result in comparatively minor punishments being meted out by sport officials. Only rarely does the legal system see fit to involve itself in cases of aggression among athletes. The reference here is, of course, to aggression that occurs outside, and in violation of, the official Rules of Play. Within the rules aggression in sports such as boxing is entirely acceptable and obviously, is what the sport is all about.

The second point concerns the matter of definition. The term "aggression" has been used somewhat carelessly to describe social behaviors that would more accurately be referred to as assertiveness or dominance. Similarly, energetic or hard-driving play is just that, energetic and hard-driving. It does not necessarily involve acts of aggression. To ensure that we are all using the term in the same way, it is perhaps useful that we keep a definition in mind throughout the upcoming sections. One that meets with the general approval of most active researchers identifies aggression as "... any form of behavior directed toward the goal of harming or injuring another living being who is motivated to avoid such treatment" (p.7).[6]

In keeping with the over-arching theme of this book, the chapters in this section will identify a set of less commonly recognized factors that have been found to play a role in sports aggression. Some chapters may only confirm what you already know or suspect to be true, others perhaps, will come as something of a surprise.

76   Letting Off Steam: Does it Help?

A generally popular notion is that people come away from an argument or fight feeling somewhat less hostile than they were previously. Merely watching others behave aggressively is similarly thought to reduce aggressive tendencies among observers. It follows from this that a heated argument between a couple, if it does nothing else, will at least clear the air, the hostility having been safely vented. It also follows that we should not be too concerned that our children are watching endless hours of television, much of it violent. After all, if watching violence serves as a safety valve that allows any aggressive urges to harmlessly escape, then that is all to the good.

The idea that people who behave aggressively or watch others do so are as a result less aggressive is called **catharsis**. As with most ideas, catharsis is not new. Its origins go back at least as far as Aristotle who expressed the opinion that audiences viewing the Greek tragic drama would be purged of the very emotions they saw portrayed by the actors. Catharsis has since come down to us as a central concept in Freudian theory and in the engaging writings of ethologist, Konrad Lorenz. There would seem to be little doubt that the concept's current popularity is due in large measure to the widespread influence of these intellectual giants. But, what if somehow Aristotle, Freud and Lorenz had it wrong. What if rather than reducing aggression, witnessing aggression or

---

[6] Baron, R. A., & Richardson, D. R. (1994). *Human aggression* (2nd ed.). New York: Plenum.

behaving aggressively instead tends to increase aggression.

Despite surveys that show approximately two thirds of those questioned subscribe to some form of cathartic belief, several decades of carefully conducted research does not provide support for the notion. While studies sometimes show no effects, when a change in a viewer's aggression does occur as a result of witnessing aggression or behaving aggressively, it is almost always in the direction of an increase. Of course, sports enthusiasts are no different than the next person. Whether they are participants or merely watch combatant sports, they are just as likely as anyone else to experience an increase in hostility.

Two studies are described below to show the typical result when the notion of catharsis is formally tested. In the first, men were shown either a film clip that featured a fight-filled hockey game or a spirited, skillful play sequence from the same game with all acts of interpersonal aggression edited out. Other men in a control condition worked on a 500-piece jig saw puzzle. Half of the subjects in each condition were angered by an accomplice of the experimenter's just prior to their participation.

If some sort of cathartic mechanism was at work then we would expect the men would be less hostile and aggressive after viewing the fight-filled film. Such was clearly not the case. Those watching the fight film became increasingly hostile while those men who additionally had been angered retaliated against the accomplice with substantially greater intensity.

The second study I have chosen takes us out of the laboratory and into the real world, in this instance a hockey arena. Spectators at an especially violent hockey game were intercepted on a random basis before the game began, during the 1st and 2nd period intermissions and immediately after the game. The same procedure was followed at a relatively peaceable game. Fans' hostility rose sharply in response to their witnessing on-ice fights peaking as the 2nd period drew to a close. By contrast, hostility remained constant at the non-violent game. Again, there was no evidence of anything resembling catharsis. Instead, we see in these results and those of a vast number of other studies that where the observation of aggression results in a change in the observer's aggression, it is almost invariably in the direction of an increase.

While the foregoing pretty much relegates catharsis to the status of myth, there are conditions in which an alternative version of the concept appears to be valid and a useful tool in the hands of therapists. For example, when things go badly as they often do, it is beneficial to talk out your problems and/or openly discuss traumatic events from your past. There is good reason to believe that in addition to reducing tension, a person may as a result be less preoccupied and better able to get on with other matters. In short, calmly and constructively confronting personally troubling events is far better than keeping things bottled up inside. Letting off steam specifically in the form of anger however, will not help but in all likelihood make matters worse.

Catharsis is an issue that touches all of us. In areas where school violence is a problem, we might do well to look at the makeup of the sports and recreational programs that are in place. For parents of an overly-aggressive youngster, enrolling them in a combatant sport is apt to produce disappointing results. Finally, the next time you hear violent media content being defended on the grounds that they provide their audiences with a safety valve for their pent-up frustrations and aggressive impulses, remember this chapter.

77 An Exception of Sorts

One of the major points that I tried to emphasize in the foregoing chapter on catharsis was that actual participation in an aggressive sport or activity frequently leads to an increase in aggression. While generally this is true, there is a very interesting exception to the rule. The exception occurs in the martial arts, specifically with the practice of karate. It appears that such training can instead, lead to a reduction in the aggression of its practitioners. This reduction occurs gradually over time and it appears only with a specific form of karate.

Sociologists at Carleton University have for a number of years been studying karate enthusiasts. The senior investigator is himself an accomplished karate. Their work reveals that as students progress through the ranks of the sport, they become increasingly less aggressive. Even though they are practicing potentially lethal skills, they give every indication of being less fractious in their day to day behavior. The key point to note however, is that this result is found with traditional dojos. This form of training includes a component in which an Asian philosophical approach emphasizing inner peace and harmony plays a major role. The values imparted by such training are presumably internalized and promote non-violent means of dealing with interpersonal conflict. Although the eventual outcome for students is a lowering of their aggressive tendencies, it is unlikely that this occurs as a result of catharsis. Far more likely, the reduction of the students' aggression results from learning. The proof of this is seen in a Texas study.

Delinquent teen-age boys were assigned to one of three recreational groups. One group learned karate skills in a traditional program that included the philosophical emphasis; another group learned karate in a program that did not include the philosophical component. A third (control) group was involved in a general sports program. Over the course of the 6 month study, those trained in the traditional form of karate showed a reduction in their aggression whereas those taking the non-traditional form showed increased levels of aggression at the conclusion of the program. This latter group of boys who were not exposed to the philosophical teachings of traditional dojos also showed an increase in their delinquent activities. The potential benefits of karate training then appear to be restricted to the traditional form in which students learn non-violent means of interacting with others.

A final point. Several writers have sounded an ominous warning. It seems that many forms of the Asian martial arts have been introduced into the North American market with the philosophical foundations of the sport either downplayed or ignored altogether. As the Texas study above indicates, this development does not bode well for society.

78   A History of Hockey Violence

Apologists for the modern version of ice hockey are quick to point out that violence has always been part of the game. Interviews with oldtimers evoke graphic accounts of brawls from the good ol' days. "Why I remember when ...." and so on. Those alarmed by what they see as unacceptably high levels of player violence are not so easily convinced. Fortunately, an answer to this important question need not be left to the speculations of armchair philosophers or the fading memories of former players. The truth lies in the records of National Hockey League (NHL) games routinely published in major North American newspapers since the league's inception.

Beginning in 1930, aggressive penalties were tallied for *all* games played during that season. The procedure was repeated at five year intervals up to 1988 (recent seasons were randomly sampled). The results of this tracking procedure are shown in the Figure below (adapted from Russell, 1993).

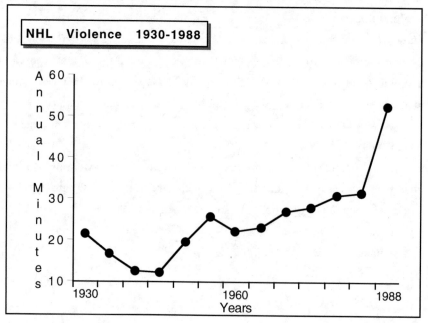

What we see are relatively low levels of player violence in the 1930-'31 season with a steady decline through the decade of the thirties and World War II until approximately 1950. At that point levels rise and continue to climb steadily until 1985 after which a further jump is seen to 1988. It should be noted that interpersonal player violence in the NHL underwent a *fourfold* increase from the immediate postwar years to 1988. The historical record of NHL violence spanning nearly 60 years clearly shows that the game can and has been played with very little interpersonal aggression. Sadly, violent elements have been allowed to redefine the sport.

79 Violence: A Winning or Losing Strategy?

While playmaking skills are generally thought to be the key to a team's success in ice hockey, some in the fraternity feel that a healthy dose of player violence makes success even more likely. Certainly, we can find examples of teams using violent tactics and intimidation winning championships. We have only to point to the Philadelphia Flyers (aka the Broadstreet Bullies) who won a second consecutive Stanley Cup championship in 1975. Where does the truth of the matter lie? Were the Flyers an exception to the rule or is player violence associated with winning championships?

The most convincing evidence I have seen on this question resulted from an examination of the records of play in the final series of the Stanley Cup. The period covered 1979-'80 through 1996-'97 during which time 90 final series games were played. Episodes of player violence, e.g., charging, fighting, kneeing, slashing, spearing, etc. were tallied for each of the two contending teams. Over the 18 year study, teams with *fewer* violent episodes won 72% of the final series (13/18). Since the 1987-'88 final, the Stanley Cup has been won by the team with the fewest violent episodes in 9 of the last 10 seasons! It does appear that encouraging player violence is a self-defeating strategy from the point of winning championships and, of course, the debilitating injuries to players that go hand in hand with violence.

80 Interracial Aggression: Between the Mound and the Plate

In Chapter 57 we saw how the number of times batters were hit by errant pitches was developed as a measure of aggression in testing the relationship between temperature and player aggression. Once again, the batter hit by pitch (BHP) measure has been used in a study, this time to track interracial aggression over the last half of the 20th century. However, before describing the results of the study let me point out an interesting sidelight to the question of BHP.

Batters in the American League (AL) are hit by pitches at a higher rate than those playing in the National League. No, AL pitchers are not an especially ill-tempered lot. Rather, the difference in hit batters originates with a rule change introduced in 1974 whereby AL pitchers do not step up to the plate. The authors of this study reason that because AL pitchers do not bat, they have no fear of retaliation and as a consequence give freer reign to their aggressive inclinations.

To return to the question of interracial aggression, Black and Hispanics were hit overall at a rate approximately 7.5% greater than were Whites for the period 1950 - 1997.[7] However, an examination of the Figure below (adapted from Timmerman, in press) reveals a more complex pattern of results including a surprising reversal in the decade of the 90s. During the decades of the 50s and 60s, Black and Hispanics were hit more often at the plate than White batters. These earlier interracial differences all but disappeared through the 70s and 80s but re-emerged in a surprising reversal in the 90s. Now we see that Whites and

---

7   The study was based on 27,002 individual player records. Across all years, 86.9% of the pitchers were White.

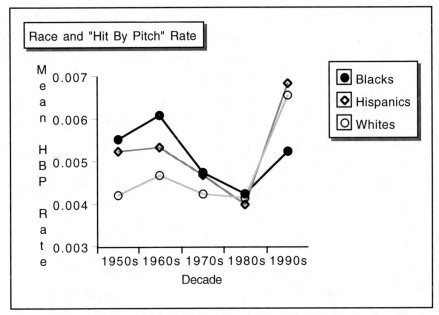

Race and "Hit By Pitch" Rate

Hispanics were hit at a higher rate than Blacks, i.e., 23% and 29% respectively. The reasons for this "reversal" are at the moment speculative.

81 Some Uniform Results

One of the underlying features of this book is that it brings to light a considerable number of findings that are surprising, sometimes even counter-intuitive. We saw earlier that the private expectations that we hold for an athlete's performance (Chapter 24), their date of birth (Chapter 2) or, their ability to estimate time Chapter 13), all have been shown to play a part in determining an athlete's eventual success. These factors are for the most part quite subtle and not commonly recognized. Even where these factors are recognized, their importance is often thought to be little more than trivial. Yet another subtle, but nonetheless powerful influence on our behavior originates with the cues to which we and others respond.

Most people recognize that posture, gestures, voice inflections, pupil dilation, etc. are effective modes of nonverbal communication. By these means we are often able to learn a great deal about another's truthfulness, mood states or intentions. Another source of valuable information is our clothing and, as we'll see shortly, its color. When our clothing is a uniform, its past associations with negative social behaviors can cause its wearer to act accordingly.

Let me set the scene. Females arrive for a study they believe is concerned with verbal learning. They are told that their job is to administer shock to another subject (actually a confederate of the experimenter) when mistakes are made in learning a word list. For reasons of wanting to minimize differences in the women's appearance, they were asked to wear a Ku Klux Klan-style costume (negative cues). As you might already have guessed, the women delivered twice as much shock to the learner when wearing the KKK uniform than did women who were not disguised and wore large name tags. Incidentally, be assured that the confederate learner did not actually receive any shocks and that this was made entirely clear to each of the women at the end of the experiment. The point then is that simply putting on clothing that has a history of associations with anti-social behaviors can cause the wearer to behave more aggressively.

One of the first decisions for owners of a new franchise is the choice of team colors. This is not a decision to be taken lightly. Color is recognized as a critical component in creating an image for the public and, of course, their opponents. Some colors convey excitement, toughness while others are based on geographical features of the franchise city, i.e., sand and sea adopted by the Miami Dolphins of the NFL. All clubs carefully avoid colors that might convey weakness or femininity. Try to think of a sports team attired in pink uniforms! There can't be many. So, just as uniforms provide cues, so too does the color of these same uniforms.

In the case of black, I think everyone recognizes its long standing association with evil, death and generally sinister forces. Throughout the tradition of cowboy movies, the villain trying to run the poor widow and her children off their homestead invariably wore black whereas the Lone Ranger and other crime fighters principally wore white. The tradition of creating a particular public image by means of color choice is carried on today by professional sports teams. Teams seeking to impress their fans or opponents with their toughness or aggressive play choose black as the basic color of their uniforms.

The intriguing question that occurred to Cornell University researchers was whether professional football and ice hockey teams actually behave in ways that are consistent with the color of their uniforms. That is, are players wearing black, black-hearted as well? The answer was found in the penalty records of the National Football League and the National Hockey League.

The uniforms from both leagues were first classified as being either predominantly black, e.g., Los Angeles Raiders, Pittsburgh Steelers, or nonblack, e.g., Miami Dolphins, Houston Oilers. An examination of league records showed that teams at or near the top of the standings in the penalty column typically wore black. Moreover, an increase in penalties occurred after teams switched from nonblack to black uniforms. As so often happens, answering one question leads to yet another question. Now they wanted to know "why" wearing black resulted in teams being more heavily penalized. Was it perhaps because referees felt compelled to call a tighter game against teams wearing black? On the other hand, it would be just as reasonable to suggest that players wearing black actually behave more aggressively, just as the women did earlier when wearing KKK uniforms.

It seems that neither referees nor players are color blind. In a follow-up study using experienced referees, the investigators found that referees do indeed, call a tighter game against teams attired in black. But, it also appears clear that when athletes don black uniforms they revert to a more aggressive style of play. The original finding of higher levels of aggression by teams that have adopted black uniforms then, has two explanations. It results from the combination of referees' more strictly enforcing the rules, and the players themselves giving freer reign to their aggressive urges when in black. Let me add as a footnote that black-uniformed teams in the NFL and NHL had the same percentage of wins as teams wearing nonblack uniforms.

82 Goons, Enforcers and the Power of Obedience

I would hazard the guess that after Pavlov's salivating dog, Stanley Milgram's classic research program on obedience is easily the best known of any in psychology. If you have never heard of Milgram then I would guess that you have never taken an introductory psychology or sociology course (or if you have, slept through it), never read Milgram's book or the Sunday supplement of your local newspaper. His work was even the subject of a feature length Hollywood movie, *The Tenth Level*, starring William Shatner. It is still shown from time to time on the late, late show.

I want to very briefly sketch his surprising findings for those who might not have been reached by media and other means. My reason for raising this topic is my belief that we continually underestimate the strength of the obedience process in accounting for anti-social behavior in sports, as elsewhere. In a sport such as ice hockey where a player is formally or informally assigned a role that places a premium on pugilistic skills, he may have little choice but to fight. The pressures to obey in most cases simply override any reluctance on the part of the athlete. The authority of a coach is virtually absolute. Disobedience can and has ended careers.

To bring everyone up to speed on Milgram's program, he found that a sizable majority of ordinary people from various walks of life went ahead and administered what they believed to be extremely high levels of shock to another individual (in actuality, the "victim" did not receive any shock whatsoever, a fact shared with each subject in the debriefing session at the conclusion of their participation). This aggression was carried out at the insistent urgings of the person in charge of running the experiment. What is important about this fact is that the person running the experiment had very little authority. In fact, the subjects were free to leave the experiment at any time and would still be paid for their participation. Now, the question we want to ask ourselves is just how obedient are people to the orders of "legitimate authority", that is, someone who actually has the power to advance or end our career? When we are told to in some way harm another person, or engage in behavior we know to be illegal or unethical, how many of us will defy the authority figure and refuse to behave in ways we know to be wrong? A study carried out in a hospital setting provides a clue.

Nurses received a phone call from a man who identified himself as Dr. X requesting that they administer 20 mg. of a drug to his patient. Although the request violated standard hospital procedures, he said that he wanted the drug to take effect by the time he arrived at the hospital at which point he would officially sign the order. The drug itself was known to be potentially lethal and indeed, a warning on the label said that the dosage should not exceed 10 mgs. Of 22 nurses who received the call from Dr. X, 21 dutifully proceeded to follow his orders being restrained only at the last minute by the researchers (in each case the dangerous drug had earlier been replaced by an inert solution). Certainly, aggression occurs because people are frustrated or because they see it modelled on television or elsewhere. However, we should not lose sight of the fact that a substantial amount of sports aggression is also in direct response to the dictates of those holding positions of authority. It seems that we are much more obedient to those in positions of power than we might otherwise have imagined.

83 "Why Me...... Why MEeeeeeeeeeeeeeee...?"

The scene that unfolded before millions of figure skating fans as they sat in front of their television sets watching the US National Figure Skating Championships was unprecedented. Nancy Kerrigan was wailing in pain and anguish at what appeared to be a serious injury to her leg inflicted by a bystander who immediately fled the arena. A strong favorite to win the womens' championship, her chances now dimmed sharply in light of her crippling injury. However, her doctors patched her up and the plucky skater went on to win the US crown and months later, Olympic silver.

The police investigation that followed the incident revealed that a boy friend of a co-competitor had made the attack on Kerrigan. Tonya Harding, a rival of Nancy's, was alleged to have instigated the assault with a view to clearing her path to the title. The skating world was in shock and disbelief. How could anyone do such a terrible thing? Is winning that important? Was it an isolated incident or, heaven forbid, could it happen again? The answer may surprise you.

Social scientists already know that more than two-thirds of the general public have had homicidal fantasies while an estimated 10% openly state they would willingly murder someone they thoroughly hated under a guarantee of anonymity and freedom from retaliation or prosecution. But these are special circumstances involving a potential victim who is thoroughly hated, not a victim who merely stands in the way of a title. We hasten to add that undoubtedly few of these people actually act on their intentions. However, some do.

To return to our figure skating incident, how many Tonya Hardings are there among athletes and sports fans? In our example, the intent was overwhelmingly to affect the outcome of the contest by removing the odds-on favorite from the competition. Is it possible that winning is that all-fired important? It seems it is that important, even to fans who are only indirectly involved in a competition through their identification with an athlete or team.

Students at Murray State University were asked if they would assault the star player or coach of the University of Kentucky mens' basketball team under a specific set of conditions. For example, the students were asked to indicate their level of agreement with "If I could remain completely anonymous and there was no possibility of arrest or retaliation, I would break the leg of the star player/coach of the opposing team immediately prior to the championship game, thereby injuring them so that they could not participate"(Wann et al., 1999). Fully 32% expressed at least some willingness to break the leg of the University of Kentucky coach while 48% were willing to injure their rival's star player by tripping him.

We might ask how the minority of students willing to commit these criminal offenses differ from those who "definitely would not" consider taking such actions. It seems that they are to be found among the Murray State fans who most highly identify with their team. Those whose self-concepts are closely tied to the fortunes of their university team are especially willing to resort to extreme measures to assist the team and in the process preserve their view of themselves as loyal fans.

84   Boxing, Football and Homicide

Football is an inherently violent game. Millions of North Americans share vicariously in that violence either as spectators in the stands or in front of their television sets. Can that exposure in any way affect their behavior in the hours or days following the game? In the case of National Football League playoff games, the answer is "yes".

Given that there is a virtual consensus among social scientists that the observation of violence generally leads to increases in viewer aggression, it was reasonable to suggest that homicide rates would increase following football games. To test the prediction, all NFL playoff games including Superbowl games, from 1973 to 1979 were examined, as were homicide rates for the metropolitan areas in which the franchise teams were located.

Homicides did indeed, increase. However, the jump in homicides occurred consistently 6 days after the playoff game. Furthermore, the rise occurred only in those franchise cities whose team had lost in the playoffs 6 days earlier. But this intriguing result deserves closer scrutiny. Why 6 days?

The sixth day following a playoff game takes us to the eve of the next round of the playoffs. Last week's winner is still in contention. By contrast, fans of last week's losing team are confronted with the realization that "their" season is over. There will be no game tomorrow, only a void. It may be that for some fans having their hopes so cruelly dashed is but one more frustration in a series of frustrations. One result of being severely thwarted can be interpersonal aggression. Additionally, we cannot rule out the possibility that the frustrations arising from gambling losses played a significant role in bringing about the jump in homicides.

Equally illuminating is a media study of professional boxing by David Phillips of the University of California at San Diego. Again we will see that the selection of those who later become victims is far from a random process and may be determined by the outcome of an athletic contest. Phillips' measure of interpersonal aggression in society was official death certificates that provide a number of basic pieces of information, including age, sex, race and the cause of death.

During the weeks leading up to and following heavily televised heavyweight championship prizefights, he tracked the rates of homicides within the viewing area. What was observed was an increase in the rate of homicides, a rate that peaked 3 days after the bout. Especially intriguing is the finding that the homicide victims bore a striking resemblance to the loser of the match. For instance, when a White contender lost to a Black boxer there was an increase in homicides among young, White males. On the other hand, an increase in homicides among young, Black males occurred when a White boxer defeated a Black opponent. Equally intriguing is the unanswered question of whether the murderers perhaps resembled the winners of the fights. Regardless of our preferred explanation for these tragic outcomes, we are left with strong evidence that the staging of professional football and boxing events has lethal implications for the general public.

85 The Long Arm of Sport Violence

The connection between watching violent sports and the tragic real-life consequences that sometimes follow is seen in two studies, the first of which involved football. For some in the Washington, D.C. area, Redskins games do not end with the final whistle. The emergency wards of area hospitals report increases in admissions of women in the categories of stabbings, gunshot wounds, assaults and "accidental" falls in the hours following the games. For reasons that are as yet a matter for speculation, the increases occur only after Redskins victories. The leading explanation for home team wins being followed by an increase in anti-social behavior involves power motivation. Fans derive an increased sense of personal power from observing their favorite team emerge victorious. The resulting increase in power motivation finds violent expression in interpersonal relationships in which disagreements that might otherwise be resolved by negotiation and compromise are instead settled by force.

To this point, a good case can be made for violent sporting events having harmful, even deadly, effects on the public at large. The previous chapter on homicides and the study described above clearly support such a conclusion. However, the case is somewhat weakened in light of recent investigations looking at the impact of professional sports on the incidence of domestic violence and child abuse.

In the first study, the records of the Los Angeles County Sheriff Department were examined for a 3-year period during which time police units were dispatched in response to 26,051 domestic violence calls. Several intriguing increases in dispatches were observed over two seasons of football, especially during the 1993-'94 season. On football Sundays dispatches increased 100% from the previous Wednesdays while the playoffs saw a 147% increase. During Superbowl week there was a whopping 264% increase in units dispatched on domestic violence calls. In the following season 1994-'95, there was, if anything, a decrease in domestic violence calls on these occasions. Incidentally, Super Bowl Sunday was not a day marked by record setting rates of domestic violence. In

1993 it ranked 23/365 while in 1994 and 1995 it ranked 11th and 96th respectively.

Although it may not be apparent to many of my readers, I must hasten to emphasize that the trends noted above are not significant and cannot be regarded as anything more than due to chance. This study therefore failed to offer support for the proposition that domestic violence is affected by professional football games.

In the second study, the records of the State of Missouri Division of Family Services Child Abuse and Neglect were examined for 1992. Rates of physical child abuse were analyzed with regard to days on which the St. Louis Blues of the National Hockey League played their regular season games. Rates were further examined in regard to home games, whether the Blues won or lost and, in regard to national playoff games in basketball, baseball, football and hockey. In none of these analyses was there any indication of a relationship with male-perpetrated child abuse on the day of the contests or the following day.

How far do violent professional sports reach into communities? Certainly, studies to date show that serious harmful effects are associated with the staging of these events. However, it remains for future studies to pinpoint the limits of that harm and to identify the conditions under which it occurs.

86 Are Athletes More Likely to Rape?

Hardly a week goes by that we don't learn of a battery or sexual assault by a member(s) of an athletic team. When allegations are made against celebrity-athletes, the event is headline news for the weeks and months that follow. It is easy to understand why the massive publicity given to such stories would lead one to think something is terribly wrong in the sports world.

In recent years, speculation has raged in both the popular press and academic writings suggesting that all-male sports groups foster attitudes that cause their members to be disproportionately represented in rape statistics. The same speculations have been levelled at military personnel and fraternities, both of whom have received more than their share of adverse publicity in recent years.

Is there good evidence to support these claims? First, studies addressing the question are few in number. Those that have investigated the question offer little if any support for the proposition that athletes are overrepresented in actual sexual assaults against women. Studies have generally been conducted on college campuses where reports of sexual assault are tallied for the general student population and compared to those of student athletes and fraternity members. While a 1993 study found a significant but weak relationship between athletic participation and rape, other studies have not confirmed that result. Taken together, the results of these studies offer only thin support for the view that athletes are any more likely than the rest of the male population to commit rape.

In an interesting sidelight, fraternity members stand apart from other campus males in the tactics they use to pressure women to have sex. Unlike athletes and other campus males, fraternity members gain compliance through verbal coercion and the use of alcohol.

The persistent notion that all-male living arrangements tend to foster rape-supportive attitudes toward women and lead to a greater incidence of rape has also been tested. To everyone's surprise, males living in mixed-sex housing rated the likelihood of their committing rape significantly higher than students in all-male housing.

A major conclusion to be drawn from these early studies is that educational programs and other means of reducing the incidence of rape should probably be directed at the general population of males. The tactic of specifically targeting athletes is likely misguided.

87 Booze and Unruly Fans

Alcohol may not deserve its reputation as a leading cause of public disorders at sports events. On those relatively rare occasions when violence erupts, sport and law enforcement officials look for causes. If alcohol is available to spectators or in any way involved it quickly becomes the prime suspect, especially if it has been consumed by young males. Other reasons are quietly pushed aside. People are more than willing to blame alcohol for disruptive behavior. Everyone knows that alcohol and some people (usually read "young males") are a dangerous mix. However, our own experience should tell us that the picture is more complicated.

On the one hand, we sense that some people become more belligerent and hostile as they consume larger and larger amounts of alcohol. At the same time, we are reminded of countless other occasions when alcohol has served as a social lubricant. At most parties there is an initial awkwardness that gradually gives way to friendlier interactions. Partygoers generally become more mellow, not hostile, as the evening wears on. This is not however, to give alcohol a clean bill of health. We are all too familiar with the tragedy of alcoholism and the continuing carnage on our highways. Nonetheless, a number of research findings are available that can provide a more accurate picture of alcohol's role in interpersonal aggression.

The first consideration to note is the degree of threat that is present in a situation. Recall for the moment the example of the typical party where a friendly, sociable climate prevails. Under such non-threatening conditions, people become intoxicated and the atmosphere remains friendly. However, introduce an element of threat and the situation is likely to turn ugly. One female guest is seen to be flirting outrageously with several husbands. Jealousy being what it is, we can expect a heated exchange at the very least. In any event, the party is probably over. Thus, intoxicated individuals who are angered or in some way threatened lash out with considerably more aggression than others who are sober. It would appear that if threat can be minimized at sports events, alcohol can be consumed without appreciably increasing the likelihood of a disturbance.

Another distinction that should be made is between beer and hard or distilled alcohol. Their effects on aggressive behavior are quite different. Whereas the consumption of brewed beverages such as beer may somewhat increase the likelihood of disorders, the consumption of distilled spirits, e.g., vodka, bourbon, results in substantially more aggression. So, when speaking about how alcohol might contribute to public disorders, it is important to keep in mind that beer is a considerably weaker cause of aggression than distilled beverages.

Why though, would distilled spirits lead to more aggression than an equivalent amount of beer? Several explanations have been proposed to account for the apparently weaker influence of brewed drinks. One explanation draws attention to "cultural expectations". By this line of reasoning, different marketing strategies for the two types of beverages have resulted in entirely different images being created for the products. Decades of advertisements for beer have featured themes of fun and good times. By contrast, distilled liquor has long standing associations in advertising and the movies with tough, macho super-males, not the sort of people you want to mess with. This explanation then, suggests that drinkers act in ways that are consistent with how the culture says they should act under the influence of brewed and distilled beverages. Beer drinkers then, are sociable; whiskey drinkers are he-men who generally let their fists do the talking.

One further point deserves mention. It has generally been assumed that when a person is intoxicated and looking to start trouble, it is virtually impossible to persuade and reason with them. Their thought processes are presumed to be so muddled that attempts to dissuade them fall on deaf ears. We now have good reason to believe that such is not the case. Evidence suggests that intoxicated persons are open to reason and can foresee the consequences of their behavior. This opens up the further option of having stadium personnel specifically trained as intervention specialists who can step into developing altercations. On the basis of what we know to this point, tactful interventions by third parties would more often than not meet with a successful resolution. Efforts along these lines are certainly preferable to the alternative, and I should add, less costly to participants to an altercation and the image of a sport. While the availability of beer may attract unruly elements to a sports event, beer consumed in friendly circumstances does not itself increase the likelihood of a crowd disturbance to any alarming degree.

Summary

The special topics discussed above represent but a smattering of the issues that are involved in questions of interpersonal aggression. Even so, several important implications can be drawn. The daily newspaper, television or even our own experiences confirm the fact that violence has crept into a number of sports that were previously played in a more peaceable vein. Whether the violence has involved the athletes or erupted among elements in the crowd, the results have been unsettling for sport officials as well as most followers of the particular sport. As with most real world problems, solutions are generally difficult to come by.

As we have seen, reliance on some sort of cathartic draining of aggressive impulses as a result of player or fan violence is wishful thinking. In fact, matters are apt to worsen. In this section and elsewhere, a long list of factors can be seen to increase the likelihood of interpersonal aggression. Whether it is the color of uniforms, alcohol or players acting on the orders of coaches, society appears unwilling to introduce strong measures to neutralize these and numerous other influences. Short of effective rule changes and a more socially responsible media, there remains a great deal that could be done at the beginning levels of a sport to head off later aggressive behavior. The values of sportsmanship, cooperation, fair play and respect for other competitors can be instilled in youngsters by understanding parents and coaches. It is not an easy task by any means. However, it is a challenge that should be met if sports are not to deteriorate to the level of brawls. Readers interested in gaining a fuller understanding of the causes of violence and its control in society are referred to the Baron and Richardson text below.[8] It provides an excellent background to the topic.

---

[8] Baron, R. A., & Richardson, D. R. (1994). *Human aggression* (2nd ed.). New York: Plenum.

XIII. Fans

Introduction

Perhaps it is not necessary for me to rush to the defence of sports fans following the previous section on violence. Even so, I will. All but a few fans conduct themselves in a civilized fashion and virtually all sporting events are staged without violent disruptions. For the most part, it is a handful of individuals who ferment trouble, grab the headlines and on rare occasions cause destruction to property, injuries and deaths. Against that background, it is easy to lose sight of the fact that those packing the stands at our major spectator sports are being entertained, socialise with others and appreciate the performances of highly skilled athletes.

The chapters to follow highlight the role of fans as they influence, and in turn are influenced by, teams in competition. Two later chapters identify the handful of fans who stand ready to instigate crowd disturbances and still others who are prepared to step in and quell any hostile outbursts. Finally, we review the chain of events that led up to the famous Soccer War in Central America followed by a description of hooliganism on the African continent.

88 As the team Goes, So Go its Fans

Spectators at many sports get thoroughly involved in a contest, attempting to influence the outcome by cheering for the home team and heckling the visitors. What is not always recognized is that the outcome of the contest can in turn, influence these same spectators in important ways. When for example, our team loses, most fans are disheartened, a few are plunged into the depths of despair. Our perceptions of the contest are also subject to distortion. Fans of the losing team are more likely to see poor officiating and dirty play by the opposition as the reason for their downfall, a view not shared by fans of the winning team. On the other hand, those identifying with the winning team can experience a short lived exaltation and surge of power motivation that can last for as long as two hours. Other changes resulting from observing one's team triumph are seen in the ways we interact with one another.

The relationship between fans and their team is quite fickle. Fans seek to share in victories, exhibiting a strong tendency to draw closer or strengthen ties to their team. This tendency is referred to as basking in reflected glory or, the BIRG effect. However, there is also a corresponding tendency for the average fan to put some distance between himself and the team when they suffer a defeat. This reaction to a loss is called CORFing or, cutting-off-reflected-failure.

For evidence that BIRGing actually follows a team victory, we have only to look at the wearing apparel worn by college students on Monday mornings. On campuses across America, students have been found to wear team-related apparel, e.g., scarfs, sweaters, following a weekend victory by their team. By contrast, on Mondays following a weekend loss, students have apparently left these items hanging in their closets.

But victories can also produce other changes in the behaviors of a loyal following. Students' choices of pronouns in describing the weekend college game are similarly influenced by whether the team won or lost. Students contacted by phone were asked if they knew the outcome of the weekend game. In providing the details of a loss, the students typically used the impersonal pronoun form, i.e., "they lost to _____ 33 to 21". By contrast, the personal pronoun "we" was used in describing a victory. That is, "we beat _____ 40 to 18".

Being associated with the failure of others is seldom a welcome prospect. Just as fans seek to share in the triumph of their team, they also take steps to put some distance between themselves and their team when their team suffers defeat. So, while we can talk of fans BIRGing when their team wins, we can also speak of CORFing, i.e., cutting off reflected failure, when they lose. For other fans however, their devotion to their team goes much deeper.

Truly dedicated fans are described as having formed a unit relationship with their team. For them, the option of CORFing is not available. That option is only available to "fair weather" fans, i.e., those with looser ties. In effect, while loyal and dedicated fans share in their team's triumphs, they must also share in the agony and suffering associated with their team's losses. The true fan stands to lose a great deal; perhaps even more than they stand to gain. As has been observed: "...it appears as though the process of forming a strong allegiance to a team is a risky venture" (Hirt et al., 1992, p. 737).

Team losses reach far beyond sports to influence aspects of fans' lives that have little or nothing to do with sports. For example, in the months prior to hostilities breaking out in Operation Desert Storm, students at Alabama and Auburn universities watched their teams play in the annual "Iron Bowl", a longstanding football rivalry. In the aftermath of a loss, the Auburn students underwent a change in their perception of threatening events in the Middle East. Asked to estimate the chance that there will be a war between Iraq and the Allied forces, Auburn students judged the prospect of war to be greater than did the Alabama students. When asked to estimate casualties, the Auburn students predicted both more Allied and Iraqi battlefield deaths than did fans of the Alabama team. Estimates of the wounded followed a similar pattern with the Auburn fans predicting greater numbers on both sides.

Other aspects of the true fan's life are also touched in important ways. University of Wisconsin males viewed broadcasts of their basketball team in competition. Following defeats, the men predicted less success for themselves and the team. Estimates of personal success in the future were seen to be lower on physical (shooting baskets in a miniature game) and mental tasks (solving anagrams). By contrast, fans of the winning team, asked to rate the response of gorgeous women to their request for a date, thought they would be more successful than those who had witnessed the defeat of their team.

Not surprisingly, one's mood and self-esteem can also take a beating as the result of a team's loss. It does however seem that it is specifically the damage to the self-esteem of dedicated fans that leads them to make lower estimates of the team's and their own future success following a loss. Certainly, moods rise and fall in the wake of a victory or defeat. But, it is the resulting changes to self-esteem that apparently underlies BIRGing (increased self-esteem) and CORFing (lowered self-esteem). The costs of dedicated fanship then, are far from trivial.

Indeed, the results of a major study suggest "...that the costs incurred from association with a losing team are much greater than the benefits accrued from association with a winner" (Hirt et al., 1992, p. 737).

It is clear from the foregoing that the outcome of athletic contests can produce changes in our attitudes, moods, expectations of personal success and even what we decide to wear on a particular day. For the most part, these represent fairly important changes that can affect the quality of our day to day interactions with others. When a team wins, the effects on fans are generally positive. But, in the case of a loss by a favorite team, just how serious are the implications for the personal well-being of fans? Certainly, some people are hit hard by a loss. They may be plunged into the depths of despair, at least for a time. The question however, is whether a goodly number of fans do not bounce back from a loss and as a consequence seek psychiatric help for stress-related illnesses such as depression? Or, is the impact of a team loss simply too weak to increase the frequency with which fans visit a psychiatric facility?

It was at the University of Michigan that researchers sought to shed some light on the question. Records of weekly attendance at the psychiatric clinic on campus provided the means to examine the rise and fall of student needs for psychiatric services. The researchers took into account considerations such as winning versus losing, home versus away games and "big" games versus those thought to be less important to the student body (big games for University of Michigan football fans are those played against their arch rivals, Ohio State and Michigan State). Taking these and other factors into account, the investigators could not find any indication that the number of people seeking help at the psychiatric clinic was in any way influenced by the success or failure of University of Michigan teams. Their conclusion was based on an examination of the records of both football and basketball for a five-year period from the 1976-'77 through the 1980-'81 seasons. Thus in the general case, it appears that the distress experienced by die-hard fans is short-lived and is not sufficiently acute to require clinical treatment. As the authors conclude, the performance of university teams appears unrelated to psychiatric clinic usage.

89 Football Weekends on Campus

With the arrival of Fall, the Saturday afternoon football game becomes a focal point for social activities on most college campuses. Across the US, students, alumni and townspeople strongly identify with their team, the more so where teams have winning records. To no one's surprise, emotions run high on football weekends.

While college administrators welcome the revenues generated by a successful football program, they are also painfully aware of the problems created for campus security personnel. The exuberant behavior of fans is seldom confined to the stadium and frequently spills over into other areas of the campus community, sometimes with destructive consequences.

To assess the impact of football weekends on campus life, the records of unruly student behavior in the residence halls on a large southeastern university were examined for a 4-year period. An overall measure of disruptive behavior included acts such as disorderly conduct, destruction of property, assaults and alcohol violations. Parenthetically, of all disciplinary incidents that were reported, 47.5% involved the possession or consumption of alcohol.

Football weekends were marked by a greater number of disciplinary cases than weekends when the team was idle. Disorderly behavior in and around the residence halls was also more frequent when the team played at home rather than away. However, whether or not the games were televised had no bearing on the number of reported incidents. Perhaps the most intriguing finding of all was that disciplinary incidents were far more frequent during the celebrations following a victory.

Why might a home team victory be more likely than a loss to trigger disorderly and destructive behavior among the student body? One explanation draws attention to the heightened sense of personal power experienced by fans witnessing their favorite team emerge victorious. Thus, disputes and grievances that normally are resolved by negotiation and compromise are instead more likely to be settled by force and anti-social behaviors.

90 Do Others "Do As I Do"?

While we are on the topic of crowds, I want to introduce a fascinating line of research that points out how our judgments about others can so easily be biased. When for example, we find ourselves seated with thousands of other spectators at a sports event we get quite clear impressions about whether everyone is enjoying themselves, how enthusiastic the crowd is, how disappointed fans became over a home town loss and so on. But, just how accurate are our estimates regarding the crowd? Is there a built-in bias when people for example, judge the motives of others in the crowd? The results of research on what has been called the **false consensus effect** indicate the answer is a resounding "yes".

What we see is a curious tendency for people to see others as having attitudes, motives, intentions, etc., that are similar to theirs. For example, if a fan wants to see a coach with a losing record fired, he and others with the same opinion will estimate that a higher percentage of the club's following feel the same way than will fans who believe the coach should be retained. It is this tendency to see others as more similar to ourselves in matters of judgment that lies behind the false consensus effect. However, there are potentially serious implications for the behavior of sports crowds arising from this type of judgmental bias.

Consider the male fan who is able and willing to join in a fight or other disturbance should one erupt in the stands. If asked for his estimate of how many other males would also join in under these circumstances, his estimate will be substantially higher than the estimates given by those who would stay clear of the disturbance. In other words, he perceives there to be an excess of like-minded males with similar intentions in the crowd. These higher estimates by those who would join in when a fight erupts have in fact been found among hockey fans in a series of studies. What this suggests is that those predisposed to involve themselves in a disturbance will be emboldened by their view that many others would take the same action. That is, they see the involvement they are considering as more "normal" behavior than do others in the sports audience. In some instances, it is not unreasonable to suggest that this perceptual bias has been responsible for minor altercations escalating to serious levels.

91 Queue Counting

Tens of thousands of jubilant fans line the streets to greet their heroes at a victory parade. Thousands more throng airports and stadia to join athletes in celebration of a championship. Sometimes the celebrations begin without the athlete or team when news of a championship victory is flashed to the home town from a distant city. News reports of the celebrations that follow a championship win are almost as important as the story of the win itself. Was the crowd well behaved or were there disturbances or episodes of violence? Part of the story of course is an estimate of the size of the crowd. I'm sure you've noticed as I have that these estimates vary considerably. Sports officials or organizers usually provide the highest estimate while a reporter or chief of police judge the crowd size to be something quite different. So great are the differences that you can't help but wonder if they are all observing the same event. Just how good are people at estimating the size of crowds?

For starters, it appears that some people are much better than others at estimating the size of crowds. Beyond that, people in general tend to underestimate the size of sports crowds. Under conditions where the actual numbers are known, observers provide estimates that consistently fall short of the actual numbers known to be in attendance. Moreover, people underestimate the size of crowds irrespective of whether there is a handful of spectators in the stands, e.g., 30, or whether the stands are full, e.g., 1,000. However, there is hope for us all. It seems that even a modest amount of training in estimating crowd size can dramatically improve our accuracy.

Sports fans also find themselves estimating numbers on other occasions. Stadium officials inform the media that an additional 1,000 tickets will be put on sale at noon tomorrow (one to a customer). The result is that long lines of fans form at the ticket windows. Some fans have even camped out overnight to ensure they will get one of the prized tickets. Those near the front of the queues are all but guaranteed tickets, those further back start to have doubts and face the possibility of a bitter disappointment. In all likelihood, everyone in line has done some quick mental arithmetic that takes into account the number of queues, the number of tickets available and how many people are ahead of them. How are people's estimates of the number of fans ahead of them affected by their own position in line?

Australian football fans who lined up in hopes of getting one of a limited number of tickets to a crucial match provided the answer. A glance at the Figure below (adapted from Mann & Taylor, 1969) shows the estimates given to interviewers by fans at different points in the queues.

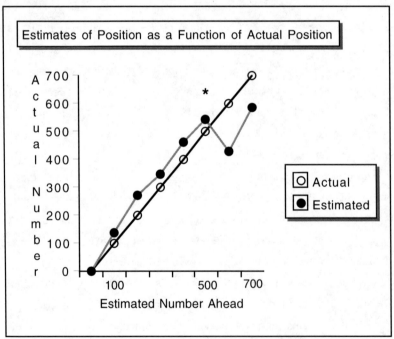

For comparison purposes, note that the solid line represents perfect estimates. What is immediately obvious is that fans standing in the front and middle sections of the line clearly overestimate the number of people ahead of them. However, fans somewhat further back suddenly begin underestimating the numbers ahead of them, a judgmental error that continues all the way back to the end of the line.

In this specific case, 2,000 tickets were to go on sale with a limit of 4 per customer. There was therefore a general recognition that the "critical" position (*) in line was approximately #500. What we see from the Figure is that the switch from overestimating to underestimating occurred very close to this point. The leading explanation for those near the front of the queue to overestimate the numbers ahead of them is that it serves as protection against the possibility, however remote, of a nasty disappointment. For those at the back of the line, underestimates provide a justification for their standing in line as well as offering reassurance that they may yet be successful in obtaining a ticket. To be sure, hope springs eternal!

92 Seeing is Believing

The question of how best to deploy police officers at sports and other types of events to minimize outbursts of violence is a critical issue in crowd control. There are two schools of thought on the issue. One view suggests that police officials have their men keep a low profile, presumably to avoid inciting elements in the crowd by their presence. The other view emphasizes the importance of positioning officers in full view of the spectators. By this line of reasoning, a show of force would discourage those among the spectators who might be tempted to engage in riotous behavior.

A Dutch researcher has given us the best answer to date. He based his conclusions on data collected at over 200 events, 80 of which involved football matches. Not surprisingly, crowd disturbances were less frequent when police were present in strength at matches rather than when fewer officers were assigned to games. However, the frequency of incidents at high risk matches was unrelated to the visibility of officers. Where a difference was found it was among the away fans. With a visible police presence, disturbances were fewer as visiting fans made their way to the stadium and later, as they left town.

The results of his study supported the old saying "seeing is believing". Stationing men in full view of football spectators appears to dramatically reduce the number of disturbances that erupt at matches as does escorting visiting supporters to and from the stadium. Positioning equal numbers of officers out of sight, just around the corner, appears to be a less effective means of crowd control. By the same token, there appears to be some truth to the further adage "out of sight, out of mind".

93   Who is Most Likely to Escalate a Riot?

How much do we know about those individuals who are likely to involve themselves in a sports riot? Several decades of research by European sociologists attempting to understand the behavior of soccer hooligans has given us a good start. A combination of observational and interview techniques has enabled them to develop a social profile of those causing disturbances in and around the football grounds. Typically, hooligans are young, single males who are irregularly employed at low paying jobs. They are further seen to be socially disaffected. That is, they have in many ways been left on the sidelines and find themselves outside the mainstream of society in terms of their culture's traditional interests and norms of behavior. While this brief sketch describes those involved in European football violence, it leaves unanswered questions of their psychological makeup.

A series of Canadian studies sought answers from men found in attendance at hockey games. Trained interviewers went into the stands and intercepted adult men following a random procedure. The key question asked of the men was their estimate of the likelihood they would join in a fight or other disturbance were one to erupt nearby in the stands. A battery of personality and other measures was administered piecemeal over the course of approximately 10 such studies. In each case there was reason to believe that the men's scores on the personality measures would be associated with their expressed willingness to escalate a crowd disturbance. For the most part, this proved to be the case.

Foremost on the list of personality traits indicative of men likely to widen the scope of a disturbance is anger and physical assaultiveness. That angry men and those with assaultive tendencies are among those most eager to do battle is hardly a surprise. What is more enlightening are the additional findings that those with an anti-social personality, a tendency to be impulsive or, sensation-seeking also appear more than willing to jump into a fight. Samples items from these last three scales will hopefully give you a feel for the trait being measured. The following will served as examples: "I often do things just for the hell of it" (psychopathy scale) "Do you look for excitement?" (impulsivity) and, "I would (*not*) like to try surf board riding" (sensation seeking).

When researchers dug into the background of the men, they found two additional factors that set rioters apart from other members of a sports audience. Would-be rioters not only had a history of fighting in the past year but also, they had fought quite recently. Further, they state that their only reason for attending hockey games is they like to watch the fights. A final distinguishing characteristic of rioters is they run in packs, i.e., they prefer to attend sporting events in the company of others.

When all of these personality and personal history factors were analyzed together in a single study, two factors emerged and overshadowed in importance all other considerations. The first was how long it had been since they last got into a fight with another man. That is, the more recently they had fought the stronger the likelihood they would escalate a disturbance. Second, those who liked to watch player fights similarly expressed a stronger willingness to join in a crowd disturbance.

To conclude, there is always a potential for hostile outbursts when people congregate. Personality traits and personal history are only part of the equation. The *situation* is all-important in determining whether or not an outburst occurs. The reason for people having come together, e.g., a picnic vs a protest, what they are observing, e.g., a badminton match vs a hockey game, environmental factors, e.g., pleasant vs oppressive temperatures; all can play a role in determining the course of events. There is a host of factors that act to facilitate aggression and at least an equal number working against outbursts of violence. For example, an irate fan may be goaded by peers to join a disturbance. At the same time, a police presence may act to restrain his tendencies to get involved. So, while some people may express even a strong willingness to escalate a riot, their words are not necessarily going to be matched by deeds.

94 Calming Troubled Waters: The Peacemakers

Those who in quarrels interpose
Must often wipe a bloody nose
The Mastiffs
John Gay (1688-1732)

We have all see film or television footage of riots whether they occurred in a political, ethnic/racial or sports setting. The events in a riot generally unfold quickly and are consequently difficult to follow. However, when it is shown in a re-run, look carefully at the various participants and you will see that individual crowd members play quite different roles. There is usually a small number of individuals actually rioting being egged on by an equally small number of rabble rousers. The majority of the people are standing around watching events unfold. But you will also notice that there is another group of individuals who can be seen physically and/or verbally trying to hold back or discourage the rioters. These are the peacemakers.

The number of peacemakers estimated to be in a sports audience range from 26.2% in a sample of Finnish males attending a hockey game to 15.4% in a sample of US college males to 17.8% in a Canadian university sample. As shown in the Figure below (adapted from Wann et al., 2001), these people are plentiful and represent an unofficial force for crowd control alongside police and

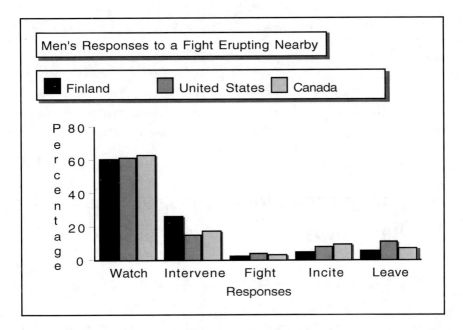

Men's Responses to a Fight Erupting Nearby

Finland   United States   Canada

security personnel. They are already on the scene, probably know the instigators and the events leading up to the hostile outburst and possibly, can snuff out a disturbance in its earliest stages.

As with rioters (see Chapter 93), we know a fair amount about those individuals who would join in a crowd disturbance in an attempt to defuse the situation. For starters, they are men who typically are of greater stature than those causing the disturbance. Furthermore, peacemakers are subject to the false consensus effect believing that an inflated number of other audience members are also ready to act as peacemakers (see Chapter 90). However, two additional features overshadow the foregoing in predicting which people in a sports audience will step forward to discourage trouble-makers.

First, they are individuals who have intervened as peacemakers in the past and who see their previous interventions as having been in some way "successful". Finally, these people hold strong convictions regarding the importance of law and order. They believe the public has a responsibility to support police agencies and hold police personnel in high regard, including advocating a career in law enforcement.

Still, you have to wonder why do they do it. When peacemakers jump into a fight, they risk serious physical and legal consequences. Police called to quell a riot do not distinguish the good guys from the bad guys. Neither is the judge apt to be sympathetic to their explanation that they were only trying to break up the fight. The result is that peacemakers with the very best of intentions will likely be sharing accommodations with the rioters in the local lock-up.

95 Soccer and Politics: Latin American Bedfellows

"The list of governments that have fallen or been overthrown by the army after the defeat of the national team is lengthy. Players on the losing side are denounced in the press as traitors to the nation" (Kapuscinski, 1986, pp. 48-49). Such is the passion for soccer in Latin America. In a part of the globe that "... is brimming with dramatic tensions", that is a "...powder keg ... chock-full" and where "...any spark will suffice to set off the conflagration" (Kapuscinski, 1986, p. 47), the outcome of international soccer matches can play a decisive role in the politics of a country. Just as governments are more secure in office when their national team wins, losses are sometimes followed by the downfall of a government. Latin economies are similarly affected by the outcome of matches. Janet Lever cites the results of a Brazilian study that revealed a 12.3% increase in production in San Paulo when the local team wins. When the same team loses, industrial accidents increase by 15.3%.

The most dramatic example of soccer's influence on Latin politics took place in 1969. It occurred on the eve of the World Cup to be staged in Mexico City. Honduras and neighboring El Salvador were playing for the right to compete in Mexico City in 1970. The first of three matches was held in the Honduran capital of Tegucigalpa. The hotel where the Salvadoran team was staying was surrounded by Honduran fans who kept up a constant din of horn honking, fire crackers and hostile chants throughout the night. The next day, a bleary-eyed

Salvadoran team lost 1-0.

Meanwhile back in San Salvador, another event stirred Salvadoran passions and drove anger to further heights. A despondent, 18-year old girl watching the winning goal on television took her father's pistol from a desk and shot herself through the heart. Her suicide galvanized the national mood. Her funeral was televised nationally. An army honor guard led the procession while the President, his Ministers and the Salvadoran team walked behind the flag-draped coffin.

Thus, the scene was set for the re-match in San Salvador. Now it was the Hondurans' turn to spend a sleepless, pre-match night. Screaming fans smashed the hotel windows and threw in dead rats and rotten eggs. A weary team rode to the stadium in armored vehicles. The stadium itself was encircled by army personnel while the soccer pitch was ringed by National Guard troops armed with submachine guns at the ready. The Honduran flag was publicly burned and in its place a filthy, tattered dishrag was run up the flagpole. Predictably, El Salvador won the match 3-0.

Violence spread in the aftermath of the victory. Whereas the Honduran team made it safely to the airport in armored cars, their fans were less fortunate. Two died and many were hospitalized as the result of beatings inflicted as they fled to the border. One hundred and fifty of their cars were put to the torch. Hours later, the border between El Salvador and Honduras was closed.

The following day a bomb fell on the Salvadoran capital and a full scale war was underway. What became known as the Soccer War lasted 4 days and claimed 6,000 lives (2,000 by another estimate) and in excess of 12,000 wounded. Entire villages were destroyed and 50,000 people lost their homes. The war ended when other Latin American countries intervened politically in the dispute, referring the matter by mutual agreement to the World Court in The Hague.

I am pleased to report that there was an eventual decision in the case. The Dutch court handed down a decision in this especially complex and long standing dispute that involved land, island and maritime boundaries. Honduras was awarded two-thirds of the territory in question. There was a further ruling that both countries share the Gulf of Fonseca with neighboring Nicaragua (It was this same Gulf that was secretly mined by the CIA in 1983 during the Reagan administration). One can only hope that having reached an honorable settlement, a measure of peace will be brought to this troubled region.

It cannot be said with any degree of certainty that the soccer games actually "caused" the war. It may have been only the last in a long series of grievances extending back over several decades. Nonetheless, it does demonstrate that sports played at an international level can be centrally involved in deadly consequences. In particular, it should be noted that federal governments have lethal military options at their disposal, options not generally available to provincial or state governments. When tensions rise, fuelled by crushing defeats in sports competition, those deadly options can and have, as we have just seen, been exercised.

96 Hooliganism in Black Africa

Soccer hooliganism is not new to the African continent. It would appear that matches are marred by violence with about the same frequency as those played in Europe and Latin America. As in the Latin American experience, actions by disruptive elements have occasionally escalated to international levels. Attacks on visiting players and rival fans in what begins as a "friendly" international match shortly draws critical comment from government sources. If deaths/injuries are numerous, the government response is decidedly stronger. We saw in the previous section that just such an event sparked a full scale war between Honduras and El Salvador. Similar events on the African continent have also set nations on a path toward armed conflict. However, Africa's version of a soccer war fortunately stopped just short of gunfire. Allow me to describe the events that nearly led to Cameroon and Gabon breaking off diplomatic relations.

It all began when a referee was about to penalize players on both teams for unnecessary roughness. Players converged on the referee and a full scale fight was underway. Matters became even more serious when spectators invaded the pitch. Elsewhere, crowds rioted in the Gabonese cities of Liberville and Port Gentil.

Roving mobs attacked Cameroonians killing as many as ten and injuring many more while the Gabonese police stood by making no effort to intervene.

During the height of the crisis, Gabonese students in Cameroon were ordered home, airline flights between the two countries were cancelled and there were rumors that diplomatic relations would shortly be broken off. All planes at the disposal of the Cameroon government were used to airlift approximately 6,000 of its people to safety. As in the previous Salvadorian example, a relatively minor event that should have passed without incident instead sparked a disturbance that escalated to lethal proportions.

One authority has stressed the role that the supernatural has played in soccer disturbances in Africa. He points specifically to **juju** as an occasional cause of disorders. My trusty dictionary defines juju as: "a magic charm or fetish used by some West African tribes". Amulets, talismans and various charms are believed to provide their owner with exceptional powers or alternatively, give protection. Their magical powers can cause a player to perform at the top of his game. Or, they may cast a spell on opposition players causing them to perform badly.

Sometimes the simple act of acquiring magical powers (or, obeying their doctors' orders) can lead players to personal misfortune. The Zimbabwe Football Association handed down lifetime suspensions to four players on the first division, Tongogara team. On the advice of their doctors (witch doctors), they were assured that victory would be theirs if they urinated on the soccer field before the Sunday game got underway. The Association chairman said his organization was "appalled" and threatened all clubs with "...the same wrath if they indulge in similar acts of public indecency" ("Doctors are not" 1989). Oh yes, Tongogara lost 2-0.

Juju is not however, used to explain all outcomes. Players seldom mention the juju's power when they win or if they play exceptionally well. It is only following a loss or poor performance that the opposing team's magical powers are seen to be operating. That is, players are quick to take personal credit when they experience success, citing their superior conditioning and playing skills. On the other hand, a poor showing is blamed on the opposition's juju, ignoring the greater possibility that their own lack of practice or talent brought about their downfall.

Something very similar happens with people generally. Social psychologists know this tendency as a **self-serving bias**. Just as with our African soccer players, people generally take credit for success and, at the same time blame external factors when they experience setbacks. In winning the office bowling tournament, our champion is likely to say that she was at the peak of her game rather than just plain lucky. The same bowler in a losing effort is more likely to say that she got a lot of bad breaks hitting head pins rather than her play was erratic. The effect of this tendency to blame juju or Lady Luck for our shortcomings is to provide protection for our self-image. After all, if others are persuaded to the view that our failures can be attributed to external factors, than our abilities or motivation need not be seriously questioned.

Summary

The collection of chapters in this section presents us with a picture of sports fans that is in most ways positive. We saw that identification with a favorite team puts fans on an emotional roller coaster. Team wins produce an emotional high and influence the way fans see the political and social world around them. Losses produce low emotional states and a less optimistic view of the world. We further saw that a small minority of sports spectators stand ready to escalate a crowd disturbance while a larger number are poised to intervene and attempt to quell a disturbance. The potential for riotous behavior at sports events exists worldwide. Two accounts of fan violence in Latin America and on the African continent provide insights into causes and cultural factors that contribute to hostile outbursts.

XIV. TWISTS AND TURNS OF SOCIAL COGNITIONS

Introduction

As everyday events unfold in the sportsworld we form impressions, make judgments and reach decisions based upon whatever evidence is available to us. These judgments may have to do with proposing a remedy for a losing season by the local franchise or deciding what has caused the slump in the performance of last season's star rookie. These are matters that can cause us concern such that we are drawn to make judgments and offer solutions.

Sometimes the evidence on which we base our judgments is sparse, at other times there is an overwhelming amount of evidence available. Even with a surplus of information about an event we manage to reach conclusions by sifting through whatever we have at our disposal. It is the means by which we process this information that is at the heart of social cognition.

It is not too much of a stretch to say that social cognition is concerned with how the mind works. From the pool of information we have available, which bits do we remember, how do we combine and interpret those bits and how do we analyze our "facts" to form a judgment?

Needless to say, faulty assumptions, a misunderstanding of probabilities and our own expectations can sometimes lead us astray and cause us to make judgments that are illogical or inaccurate. Throughout this section you will be introduced to illustrations of how various biasing influences can distort our judgments regarding sports events. In the initial chapter leading off this section we see an example of how the direction in which we focus our thoughts can result in a judgment that runs counter to objective facts.

97 Being Happier With Less

Who among us would not be delighted with having won an Olympic medal? Would the joy of the gold medal winner not be greater than that of the silver medalist who in turn, would experience greater joy than the bronze medalist? One would certainly expect that the joy and satisfaction experienced by Olympic champions would correspond to the color of their medal. Surprisingly, that is not the case. Even though objectively, the importance of the medals increases from bronze to silver to gold, a cognitive process called **counterfactual thinking** leads Olympians to see things quite differently.

Consider an early observation by William James (1892).

> *So we have the paradox of a man shamed to death because he is only the second pugilist or the second oarsman in the world. That he is able to beat the whole population of the globe minus one is nothing; he has "pitted" himself to beat that one; and as long as he doesn't do that nothing else counts.*
>
> (cited in Medvec et al., 1993, p. 603)

Now consider the silver and bronze medalists. The thoughts of the silver medalist are inevitably drawn upwards toward thoughts of what might have been. They were but a step away from Olympic glory and the lavish rewards typically heaped on the victor. By the standard of the gold medal then, a silver medal is somewhat disappointing. By contrast, the focus of the bronze medalist's thoughts is downwards to those competitors finishing out of the medals. From the perspective of the bronze medal winner, he/she has achieved a satisfying result. They have a medal whereas the rest of the field does not.

Because of the asymmetry in the direction of their respective comparisons, the two medalists are entertaining entirely different thoughts. The silver medalist is plagued by thoughts of "what if ...", "if only I had ...". The winner of the bronze medal in looking to the rest of the field is cheered by thoughts of having at least won a medal. Although the silver medalist is objectively better off than the bronze medalist, their focus on "what might have been" could result in their being less happy with their achievement.

To test the prediction that "less is more", i.e., that bronze medalists are happier than silver medalists with their achievements, researchers obtained clips of NBC coverage of the 1992 Barcelona, summer Olympic games. The footage captured the immediate reactions of all bronze and silver medalists as they learned of their finishing position. Additional footage was obtained showing the reactions of medalists during the awards ceremony when they were honored on the victory stand.

The immediate reactions of medalists upon learning of their finishing position and their reactions on the medal stand were rated for the degree of "happiness" by impartial judges. Be assured that the panel of judges were sports illiterates with little or no interest in sports, nor were they familiar with the athletes and their Olympic achievements.

The results of the judges' ratings (from "agony" to "ecstasy") were as predicted. The reactions of athletes upon learning that they had just won a bronze medal was one of extreme joy. Silver medalists were less joyous. The emotional reactions of those on the victory rostrum followed a similar pattern. Those presented with bronze medals reacted with greater expressions of happiness than their rivals who were awarded silver. In sum, even though a silver medal represents a greater achievement than a bronze medal, counterfactual thinking can lead to what is objectively less being seen as more.

Life's near misses haunt us all. Being first runner up in the pageant, missing an A grade by one point, losing out to your rival for the affections of your dream date, each of these disappointments can continue to gnaw at one for weeks, months or even years.

98   Are We Primed for Violence?

Are we in a very real sense made ready to behave aggressively even before we take our seats at combatant sports events? Does the language and images contained in pre-game publicity contribute to an increased likelihood of disturbances erupting among spectators? The suggestion is not far-fetched. Psychologists working in the area of cognitive processes are well aware of what are called **priming effects**. Stored memories or schema can be activated and subsequently determine the kind of judgments we make in regard to our social situation. At the risk of oversimplifying matters, if friendly cooperative schemas are activated, others in our social surroundings are likely to be seen in a positive light. On the other hand, if the content of pre-game publicity activates anti-social or negative schemas, then others with whom we come in contact are apt to be judged unfavorably or be seen as personally threatening.

The following study provides the clearest illustration of how mere words with aggressive associations or overtones can set the stage for open conflict. Students recited one of two lists of words. The first list contained the names of several non-aggressive sports, e.g., golf, bowling, billiards. The other list was identical except that the non-aggressive sports were replaced with sports having long-standing associations with aggression, e.g., boxing, football, ice hockey. Later, everyone was asked to describe an individual named Curtis. The descriptions were strikingly different. Those who earlier had recited the names of non-aggressive sports saw Curtis in a generally positive light. By contrast, students who recited aggressive sport names described Curtis as hostile and menacing. In the latter case, negatively toned schemas containing these aggressive elements were presumed to be activated and used by the students in constructing their overall impressions of Curtis.

In carrying the case for priming one step forward, it is important to recognize that we typically act on our perceptions of people quite apart from any objective facts about that person. Curtis may be a perfectly friendly and gentle person. Yet, if priming has led us to see him as hostile and threatening then our response to him will be framed in similar terms. If pre-game hyperbole (hype) has unknowingly created a hostile social climate at a sports site, then many spectators will tend to see others as looking to start trouble and as having hostile intentions. In such circumstances where the stage is unwittingly set for violence, the results on a few occasions, could be regrettable.

99 The Law of Small Numbers

When the Calgary Flames hockey club failed to advance beyond the first round of the Stanley Cup playoffs for the third consecutive year, their coach Dave King was fired. When Britain's premiere golfer, Nick Faldo failed to win a "major" title over several seasons, it was widely believed that he was prone to "choking" under the pressure of championship play. Indeed, he was dubbed "Nick Foldo" by an unsympathetic press. Is the damage to their respective reputations justified by the evidence?

The Law of Large Numbers is a cornerstone of statistical theory. Thus, an "average" is a fairly faithful reflection of all cases when a very large sample is drawn. We have good reason to trust the accuracy of statistics when they are computed from a sufficiently large number of observations. However, people appear to lose sight of the importance of sample sizes in making day to day judgments, acting as though small samples are equally informative as large samples. Not so! For example, a coach may pencil a reserve player into the starting lineup because he notes that the player has a .500 lifetime batting average against the opposing pitcher. The coach's tactic makes little sense if upon closer scrutiny we see that it is based on 3 hits in 6 times at bat.

It is this widespread belief in a bogus Law of Small Numbers that can earn coaches and players undeserved reputations for failure. David King came up short on 3 occasions and despite coming close, Nick Faldo failed to win a major tournament title during several seasons of play. In both instances the number of observations is exceedingly small, certainly too small to conclude that Messrs.

King and Faldo lack the skills necessary for success in their professions. Unfortunately, a deep-seated belief in the Law of Small Numbers by fans, sportscasters and franchise owners has caused damage to reputations and sometimes, a loss of employment.

100   Thoughts of a Racetrack Bettor

Do you remember how you felt minutes after making a final choice from among several attractive alternatives? Were you not momentarily gripped by uncertainty and self-doubts that you made the right decision?

Consider the purchase of a car. The moment you sign the sales contract, a sense of possibly having made the wrong decision sets in. "Maybe I should have bought the Ford or even the Chevy instead". The technical name given to this psychologically discomforting state is **dissonance**. One means by which we can find relief from this uncomfortable mental state is to increase the attractiveness of our choice. For example, new car owners prefer to read advertisements for the car they have just purchased rather than ads for those they chose not to buy. Bettors at the race track do much the same thing.

A random sample of bettors was intercepted moments before they placed their bet at the $2.00 "win" window. They were asked to rate the chances that the horse they were betting on would win the race. A different sample of bettors was asked to make the same rating immediately after purchasing their ticket.

Those in the prebet group gave their horse only a "fair" chance of winning the race. Those interviewed immediately after placing their bets thought their horse stood a much better chance of winning, describing its chances as "good". As with new car buyers, bettors re-assess their decision in ways that increase the attractiveness of their final choice. Seeing their choice as now more attractive acts to reduce the mental anguish that follows from having made a difficult decision.

You might ask if perhaps the postbet group thought their horse had a better chance because they changed their minds seconds before laying down a bet, i.e., just after they had been interviewed. If a number had in fact switched and bet favorites, then certainly they would rate their horses as having a better chance. However, a check on this possibility revealed that when people change their bets at the last moment most switch to long shots, not to favorites.

The entire process by which the act of placing a wager leads to a bettor seeing his/her choice as more attractive is reflected in the comments of one prebet subject who, upon leaving the window approached a postbet interviewer: "Are you working with that other fellow there? (indicating the prebet interviewer who was by then engaged in another interview). Well, I just told him that my horse had a fair chance of winning. Will you have him change that to a good chance? No, by God, make that an excellent chance" (Knox & Inkster, 1968, p. 322).

Alas, bettors frequently lose at the track. What effect if any, do prior losses have on wagering decisions, for example, on the last race of the day? Do bettors take an increased risk in hopes of recouping their previous loss or do they generally opt for a more conservative strategy? While we might guess that those having a losing day would be more likely to bet their shirt on the final race, such is not the case. It appears instead that bettors seek *less* risk when faced with an earlier loss.

101 Cause and Effect: What Really Causes What?

We humans are continually engaged in trying to make sense of the events we encounter in our daily activities. What caused someone to behave as they did? What is the reason(s) that has propelled our favorite team to the top of the league standings? It is this constant search for causal factors that provides much of the grist for discussions among fans.

From among the dozens of potential factors, certain ones seem, more than others, to be connected to team victories. The error we commonly make is in assuming that a factor "related" to a team's winning must necessarily be causing their success. Let me illustrate. Spectators take note of the fact that when a particular star running back gets over 100 yards in a game, his team is far more likely to win than when he runs for less than 100 yards. For example, his team has won nearly all of their games (34 wins/ 2 losses) when he has carried for 100 yards or more. When his carries total less than 100 yards, their record is far less impressive (45 wins/ 26 losses). It is hard to resist the temptation to infer that the team victories were caused by the running back. To a certain extent they were. However, in this example and many others that we might cite, the case for a cause and effect relationship is considerably weakened.

What our sportscasters and fans might have noticed on closer inspection of the league's records is that in winning games our running back generally carried the ball for more yards in the second half, extra yardage that put him over the 100 yard mark. What is in fact occurring, is that teams that are ahead late in the game elect to run the ball rather than risk having a pass intercepted. This safer tactic provides the back with more opportunities for yardage. Generally, the tactic is successful in preserving the lead. Under these circumstances, it is not too difficult to see how our spectators might come to see 100 yard performances by the star running back as the cause of game outcomes. Equally, if not more likely, winning performances by the team are the cause of the star's 100 yard games.

The folly of assuming a cause and effect relationship from the fact that two factors change together can clearly be seen in an example provided by Cornell psychologist Thomas Gilovich. A 5 ft. 6 inch colleague of Gilovich's delights in reminding him that his high school basketball team won all 40 games in which he played. While we might be tempted to conclude that his vertically-challenged colleague possessed outstanding court skills, the real explanation is that the coach emptied his bench late in games in which his team had built up a commanding lead such that there was no chance of their being overtaken.

102 The Sophomore Jinx

One of the sportsworld's most popular beliefs shared by fans, sportscasters and athletes alike, is the sophomore slump. With some regularity, we see players who in their rookie year give every indication of becoming superstars of the future follow with a disappointing season in their second year. Of course, the most disappointed are those owners who signed the promising rookie to a new muti-zillion dollar contract at the end of his first year.

There is however, no shortage of explanations for the phenomenon. Some invoke a supernatural explanation and simply see the sophomore year itself as somehow jinxed. Others attempt more plausible explanations suggesting instead that the athlete has become complacent or developed an inflated opinion of himself. Still others suggest that opposing players have learned how to exploit the rookie's weaknesses in the second year. While the latter explanations may explain the rare individual case, a far better explanation is available to account for the general case, namely, **regression effects**.

Most of those with even a smattering of a statistical background recognize that those whose performance on one occasion is extreme, i.e., extremely good or extremely poor, will on a second occasion tend to perform closer to their average. For example, weekend golfers who score well below their average one week can generally be expected to score closer to their average the second week. By contrast, those scoring well above their average can be expected to slip back toward their average the following week. Similarly, a record-setting cold winter is likely to be followed by a winter with temperatures closer to the historical average for the region. Also, an unusually mild winter is apt to be followed by a winter of somewhat colder temperatures.

What we see in these examples are regression effects, the result of an imperfect correlation between two occasions when performances, e.g., golf, weather, are measured. Many extremely good (or bad) performances include a healthy measure of luck (or bad luck). For other athletes their exceptional performance reflects true ability. In any year, a number of baseball's crop of rookies have outstanding seasons. Several among them will ultimately be inducted into the Baseball Hall of Fame. Their performance in their rookie year simply reflected their true ability level. For others, their outstanding rookie performance was well above their true ability level, the result of a set of favorable circumstances, including luck. For them, a less successful sophomore season is to be expected.

This line of reasoning is supported by an examination of the performance of Hall of Famers over the course of their careers. These outstanding ball players showed no indication of anything resembling a sophomore slump. Their batting averages during their sophomore years were indistinguishable from their career averages. Seemingly, ballplayers are not jinxed in their sophomore years. Rather, having had an exceptionally good rookie year most fall back to a level of performance that more accurately reflects their true ability.

The evaluation of coaches and teams can also be biased as a result of regression effects. Teams coming off a near-perfect season can be expected to do less well next year just as cellar-dwelling teams will likely show improvement in the following season.

One common scenario sees mounting fan and media pressures for firing the coach with a string of losses. Often the coach is sacrificed to appease the fans and an interim coach appointed. The team's critics are vindicated when the new coach manages a few wins over the balance of the season. This is just what would be predicted on the basis of regression effects, improvement after a run of extremely poor showings. The team's problems may be further compounded however, when the interim coach is given a new contract. His modest success in "turning the team around" gives fans the promise of better things to come. Unfortunately, further disappointments may be in store for fans if the previous success was simply the result of regression effects.

Of course, good coaching can be effective in improving a team's fortunes. A disastrous season followed by a winning season under a new coach undoubtedly reflects effective coaching. After all, it is regression toward the mean, not beyond the mean that is implied by statistical regression.

The foregoing provides us with a straightforward and more likely explanation for these occurrences. When we see a promising rookie struggling in his sophomore year or a new coach reversing the fortunes of a cellar-dwelling club, we should first look to regression effects for an explanation. By the same token, the failure of a team to repeat a championship season does not necessarily reflect badly on their abilities or those of their coach.

103 Mind Games: Sandbagging and Self-handicapping

As an important competition draws near, some athletes make public comments designed to give them an edge or protect their reputation in the event of a disappointing performance. Two common strategies are sandbagging and self-handicapping.

Sandbagging involves the athlete demonstrating, or in some way letting it be known, that their upcoming performance will likely be substandard or less than people are expecting. By claiming that their abilities are less than they are, the athlete hopes that his/her opponent will make fewer preparations for the competition and/or make less of an effort. Notre Dame football coach Lou Holtz was well known for his use of the strategy. He is quoted as saying "We're not a good enough football team to play the people we have to play". At the time the Fighting Irish were ranked 4th in the nation and had a 5-0 record! Of course, rather than claiming less ability, one can also mislead an opponent into thinking they can win handily with a display of sub par skills. For example, the pool shark may carefully set up his victim for a large wager by first losing a few games.

Another somewhat similar strategy used by athletes to minimize potential damage to their overall reputation is **self-handicapping**. Here the athlete attempts to determine in advance how others will interpret a poor performance should that occur. For example, before a competition the athlete may mention having the flu, a twisted ankle or that they are troubled by personal problems.

Should they turn in a disappointing performance fans and others will for example, likely point to the flu as the cause, not a lack of effort or preparation. As a consequence, the athlete's reputation remains intact. However, note that a "bonus" can result from self-handicapping. Should our athlete happen to win the competition, he/she did so despite having to also fight off the debilitating effects of the flu. In the eyes of many of their fans, what was already an excellent reputation grows to even larger proportions. By all accounts the strategy is very popular among athletes, so much so that early researchers were prompted to comment that "self-handicappers are legion in the sports world" (Jones & Berglas, 1978, p. 201).

Certainly, these are not the only mind games that people play. Some overblow their own abilities while still others heap excessive praise on an opponent. The sports section of your local bookstore is chock-full of paperbacks offering advice on how to win or "psych out" your opponent. From my perspective, I would much prefer to surpass (or lose to) an opponent who is playing at the top of their game. There can be little to zero satisfaction in winning because of an unfair and deceptive advantage that you have created.

Summary

In this final section, I have introduced a number of sport-related concepts from the emerging field of social cognitions. Each provides insights into the underlying thought processes of athletes and fans as they, for example, stand on the victory podium, bet on a horse race or demand a coach be sacked. In many ways I think this is the most intriguing of the 14 sections. You may find it worth a second read.

A FEW CONCLUDING THOUGHTS

This collection was started back in 1993 during a Sabbatical year at the University of Utrecht in The Netherlands. This entire undertaking has been fun for me and my hope is that you the reader have found the book well worth the read. This is an ongoing project for me. If you have other topics or articles you feel deserve a space in a future edition, by all means bring them to my attention along with any suggestions or comments. I would be delighted to hear from you.

e-mail: russell@uleth.ca

my home page: www.ampsc.com/~grussell

My special thanks to the following friends and colleagues who have helped me along the way: Dr. Jeffrey H. Goldstein (Utrecht University), Dr. Ivan Kelly (University of Saskatchewan), Dr. Bryan Kolb (University of Lethbridge), Dr. Nicolien Kop (Utrecht University), Dr. J. W. Nienhuys (Eindhoven University of Technology), Audrey Russell, Shelley Svidal, Dr. Hal Weaver, John Zylstra.

REFERENCES
[* related readings]

I. INDIVIDUAL PERFORMANCE

1 Competition: Not All It's Cracked Up to Be

Berkowitz, L. (1962). *Aggression: A social psychological analysis.* New York: McGraw -Hill.

Helmreich, R. L., Beane, W., Lucker, G. W., & Spence, J. T. (1978). Achievement motivation and scientific attainment. *Personality and Social Psychology Bulletin, 4,* 222-226.

Helmreich, R. L., & Spence, J. T. (1978). The Work and Family Orientation Questionnaire: An objective instrument to assess components of achievement motivation and attitudes toward family and career. *JSAS Catalogue of Selected Documents in Psychology, 8,* 35. (Ms. No. 1677).

Helmreich, R. L., Spence, J. T., Beane, W. E., Lucker, G. W., & Matthews, K. A. (1980). Making it in academic psychology: Demographic and personality correlates of attainment. *Journal of Personality and Social Psychology, 39,* 896-908.

Johnson, D. W., Maruyama, G., Johnson, R., Nelson, D., & Skon, L. (1981). Effects of cooperative, competitive, and individualistic goal structures on achievement: A meta-analysis. *Psychological Bulletin, 89,* 47-62.

*   Johnson, D. W., & Johnson, R. T. (1989). *Cooperation and competition: Theory and research.* Edina, MN: Interaction.

*   Miller, A. G., & Thomas, R. (1972). Cooperation and competition among Blackfoot Indian and urban Canadian children. *Child Development, 43,* 1104-1110.

2 Handicapped by your Birthdate

Allen, J., & Barnsley, R. H. (1993). Streams and tiers: The interaction of ability, maturity, and training in systems with age-dependent recursive selection. *Journal of Human Resources, 28,* 649-659.

Barnsley, R. H., Thompson, A. H. (1988). Birthdate and success in minor hockey: The key to the NHL. *Canadian Journal of Behavioural Science, 20,* 167-176.

Barnsley, R. H., Thompson, A. H., & Legault, P. (1992). Family planning football style: The relative age effect in football. *International Review for the Sociology of Sport, 27,* 77-88.

Thompson, A. H., Barnsley, R. H., & Dyck, R. J. (1999). A new factor in youth suicide: The relative age effect. *Canadian Journal of Psychiatry, 44,* 82-85.

Thompson, A. H., Barnsley, R. H., & Stebelsky, G. (1991). "Born to play ball": The relative age effect and major league baseball, *Sociology of Sport Journal, 8,* 146-151.

3   Age and Peak Performance

Schulz, R. & Curnow, C. (1988). Peak performance and age among superathletes: Track and field, swimming, baseball, tennis, and golf. *Journal of Gerontology: Psychological Sciences, 43,* 113-120.

Schulz, R., Musa, D., Staszewski, J., & Siegler, R. S. (1994). The relationship between age and major league baseball performance: Implications for development. *Psychology and Aging, 9,* 274-286.

4   Eye Color and Racial Differences in Performance

Jones, J. M., & Hochner, A. R. (1973). Racial differences in sports activities: A look at the self-paced versus reactive hypothesis. *Journal of Personality and Social Psychology, 27,* 86-95.

Worthy, M., & Markle, A. (1970). Racial differences in reactive versus self-paced sports activities. *Journal of Personality and Social Psychology, 16,* 439-443.

* Beer, J., & Beer, J. (1989). Relationship of eye color to professional baseball players' batting statistics given on bubblegum cards. *Perceptual and Motor Skills, 69,* 632-634.

* Levin, M. (2000). *Taboo: Why black athletes dominate sports and why we are afraid to talk about it.* New York: W.W. Norton.

5   White Men Can't Jump: Black Men Can't Swim

Mael, F. A. (1995). Staying afloat: Within-group swimming proficiency for whites and blacks. *Journal of Applied Psychology, 80,* 479-490.

6   Batting Right Versus Batting Left

Grondin, S., Guiard, Y., Ivry, R. B., & Koren, S. (1999). Manual laterality and hitting performance in Major League Baseball. *Journal of Experimental Psychology: Human Perception and Performance, 25,* 747-754.

7   Two Types of Motivation

Deci, E. L., Betley, G., Kahle, J., Abrams, L., & Porac, J. (1981). When trying to win: Competition and intrinsic motivation. *Personality and Social Psychology Bulletin, 7,* 79-83.

Deci, E. L., & Ryan, R. M. (1985). *Intrinsic motivation and self-determination in human behavior.* New York: Plenum.

II. TEAM PERFORMANCE

8   The Home Field Advantage

Godden, D. R., & Baddeley, A. D. (1975). Context-dependent memory in two natural environments: On land and underwater. *British Journal of Psycho - logy, 66,* 325-331.

Greer, D. L. (1983). Spectator booing and the home advantage: A study of social influence in the basketball arena. *Social Psychology Quarterly, 46,* 252-261.

Jehue, R., Street, D., & Huizenga, R. (1993). Effect of time zone and game time changes on team performance: National Football League. *Medicine and Science in Sports and Exercise, 25,* 127-131.

Wright, E. F., Jackson, W., Christie, S. D., Mcguire, G. R., & Wright, R. D. (1991). The home-course disadvantage in golf championships: Further evidence for the undermining effect of supportive audiences on performance under pressure. *Journal of Sport Behavior, 14,* 51-60.

*   Russell, G. W. (1993). *The social psychology of sport.* New York: Springer-Verlag.

9   The Championship Choke

Baumeister, R. F. (1984). Choking under pressure: Self-consciousness and paradoxical effects of incentives on skillful performance. *Journal of Personality and Social Psychology, 46,* 610-620.

Baumeister, R. F. (1985, April). The championship choke. *Psychology Today,* pp. 48-52.

Baumeister, R. F., & Steinhilber, A. (1984). Paradoxical effects of supportive audiences on performance under pressure: The home field disadvantage in sports championships. *Journal of Personality and Social Psychology, 47,* 85-93.

*   Schlenker, B. R., Phillips, S. T., Boniecki, K. A., & Schlenker, D. R. (1995). Where is the home choke? *Journal of Personality and Social Psychology, 68,* 649-652.

1 0   When Praise Hurts

Baumeister, R. F., Hutton, D. G., & Cairns, K.J. (1990). Negative effects of praise on skilled performance. *Basic and Applied Social Psychology, 11,* 131-148.

1 1   When 2 + 2 = 3

Huddleston, S., Doody, S. G., & Ruder, M. K. (1985). The effect of prior knowledge on the social loafing phenomenon on performance in a group. *International Journal of Sport Psychology, 16,* 176-182.

Latané, B., Williams, K., & Harkins, K. (1979). Many hands make light the work: The causes and consequences of social loafing. *Journal of Personality and Social Psychology, 37,* 823-832.

Williams, K. D., Harkins, S. G., & Latané, B. (1981). Identifiability as a deterrent to social loafing: Two cheering experiments. *Journal of Personality and Social Psychology, 40,* 303-311.

Williams, K. D., Nida, S. A., Baca, L. D., & Latané, B. (1989). Social loafing and swimming: Effects of identifiability on individual and relay performance of intercollegiate swimmers. *Basic and Applied Social Psychology, 10,* 73-81.

* Karau, S. J., & Williams, K. D. (1993). Social loafing: A meta-analytic review and theoretical integration *Journal of Personality and Social Psychology, 65,* 681-706.

* Kravitz, D. A., & Martin, B. (1986). Ringelmann rediscovered: The original article. *Journal of Personality and Social Psychology, 50,* 936-941.

1 2   Who Really Won the Summer Olympics?

den Butter, F. A. G., & van der Tak, C. M. (1995). Olympic medals as an indicator of social welfare. *Social Indicators Research, 35,* 27-37.

III. SECRET INGREDIENTS OF SUCCESS

1 3   Timing is Everything

McCown, W., & Edwards, J. (circa 1987). *Time perception and thoroughbred jockeys.* Unpublished manuscript. Loyola University of Chicago.

Oki, H., Sasaki, Y., Lin, C. Y., & Willham, R. L. (1995). Influence of jockeys on racing time in thoroughbred horses. *Journal of Animal Breeding Genetics, 112,* 171-175.

1 4   Ice-bergs: Searching for the Best

Morgan, W. P., O'Connor, P. J., Ellickson, K. A., & Bradley, P. W. (1988). Personality structure, mood states, and performance in the elite male distance runners. *International Journal of Sport Psychology, 19,* 247-263.

Rowley, A. J., Landers, D. M., Kyllo, L. B., & Etnier, J. L. (1995). Does the iceberg profile discriminate between successful and less successful athletes? A meta-analysis. *Journal of Sports & Exercise Psychology, 17,* 185-199.

Wann, D. L., Inman, S., Ensor, C. L., Gates, R. D., & Caldwell, D. S. (1999). Assessing the psychological well-being of sport fans using the Profile of Mood States: The importance of team identification. *International Sports Journal, 3,* 81-90.

1 5 Leaders Who (Don't) Fold Under Pressure

Fiedler, F. E., Mcguire, M. A., & Richardson, M. (1989). The role of intelligence and experience in successful group performance. *Journal of Applied Sport Psychology, 1,* 132-149.

Fiedler, F. E., Potter, E. H., & McGuire, M. A. (1988). *Stress and effective leadership decisions.* (Tech. Rep. No. 88-3). Seattle: University of Washington.

Gibson, F. W., Fiedler, F. E., & Barrett, K. (1993). Stress, babble, and utilization of leader intellectual abilities. *Leadership Quarterly, 4,* 189-208.

* Fiedler, F. E. (1995). Cognitive resources and leadership performance. *Applied Psychology: An International Review, 44,* 5-28.

* Vecchio, R. P. (1990). Theoretical and empirical examination of cognitive resource theory. *Journal of Applied Psychology, 75,* 141-147.

1 6 Brainpower at the Racetrack

Ceci, S. J., & Liker, J. K. (1986). A day at the races: A study of IQ, expertise, and cognitive complexity. *Journal of Experimental Psychology: General, 115,* 255-266.

1 7 Optimism Wins

Peterson, C. (1995). Explanatory style and health. In G. C. Buchanan & M. E. P. Seligman (Eds.), *Explanatory Style* (pp. 233-246). Hillsdale, NJ: Erlbaum.

Reivich, K. (1995). The measurement of explanatory style. In G. C. Buchanan & M. E. P. Seligman (Eds.), *Explanatory Style* (pp. 21-47). Hillsdale, NJ: Erlbaum.

Rettew, D., & Reivich, K. (1995). Sports and explanatory style. In G. C. Buchanan & M. E. P. Seligman (Eds.), *Explanatory Style* (pp. 173-185). Hillsdale, NJ: Erlbaum.

Seligman, M. E. P., Nolen-Hoeksema, S., Thornton, N., & Moe Thornton, K. (1990). Explanatory style as a mechanism of disappointing athletic performance. *Psychological Science, 1,* 143-146.

1 8 The Winning Edge in Golf

Belkin, D. S., Gansneder, B., Pickens, M., Rotella, R. J., & Striegel, D. (1994). Predictability and stability of professional golf association tour statistics. *Perceptual and Motor Skills, 78,* 1275-1280.

Engelhardt, G. M. (1997). Differences in shot-making skills among high and low money winners on the PGA tour. *Perceptual and Motor Skills, 84,* 1314.

Jimenez, J. A. (1999). Are European and American golf players different? Reply to Engelhardt (1997). *Perceptual and Motor Skills, 89,* 417-418.

Thomas, P. R., & Over, R. (1994). Psychological and psychomotor skills associated with performance in golf. *The Sport Psychologist, 8,* 73-86.
* McCaffrey, N., & Orlick, T. (1989). Mental factors related to excellence among top professional golfers. *International Journal of Sport Psychology, 20,* 256-278.

IV. TIPS ON IMPROVING PERFORMANCE

19 Golfers' Yips

Klawans, H. L. (1996). The Bantam: Ben Hogan. In H. L. Klawans (Ed.), *Why Michael couldn't hit, and other tales of the neurology of sports* (pp. 83-108). New York: W.H. Freeman.
McDaniel, K. D., Cummings, J. L., & Shain, S. (1989). The "yips": A focal dystonia of golfers. *Neurology, 39,* 192-195.
Sachdev, P. (1992). Golfers' cramp: Clinical characteristics and evidence against it being an anxiety disorder. *Movement Disorders, 7,* 326-332.

20 Caffeine and Performance

Fisher, J. (1995). The coffee connection. *Muscular Development, 32,* 142-143.
Pasman, W. J., van Baak, M. A., Jeukendrup, A. E., & de Haan, A. (1995). The effect of different dosages of caffeine on endurance performance time. *International Journal of Sports Medicine, 16,* 225-230.

21 "The Little Engine That Could"

Bandura, A. (1986). *Social foundations of thought and action.* Englewood Cliffs, NJ: Prentice-Hall.
Bandura, A. (1990). Perceived self-efficacy in the exercise of personal agency. *Applied Sport Psychology, 2,* 128-163.

22 Larks and Owls

Baxter, C., & Reilly, T. (1983). Influence of time of day on all-out swimming. *British Journal of Sports Medicine, 17,* 122-127.
Rodahl, A., O'Brien, M., & Firth, R. G. R. (1976). Diurnal variation in performance of competitive swimmers. *Journal of Sports Medicine, 16,* 72-76.
* Reinberg, A., Proux, S., Bartal, J. P., Levi, F., & Bicakova-Rocher, A. (1985). Circadian rhythms in competitive sabre fencers: Internal desynchronization and performance. *Chronobiology International, 2,* 195-201.
* Smith, R. S., Guilleminault, C., & Efron, B. (1997). Circadian rhythms

and enhanced athletic performance in the National Football League.
Sleep, 20, 362-365.

23   Practice Makes Perfect

Hall, K. G., Dominques, D. A., & Cavazos, R. (1994). Contextual interference effects with skilled baseball players. *Perceptual and Motor Skills, 78*, 835-841.

V. THE DECISION MAKERS

24   Pygmalion on the Balance Beam

Ansorge, C. J., Scheer, J. K., Laub, J., & Howard, J. (1978). Bias in judging women's gymnastics induced by expectations of within-team order. *Research Quarterly, 49*, 399-405.

Burnham, J. R. (1968). *Effects of experimenter's expectancies on children's ability to learn to swim.* Unpublished master's thesis. Purdue University, West Lafayette, IN.

25   Judges: A Patriotic Bias?

Ansorge, C. J., & Scheer, J. K. (1988). International bias detected in judging gymnastic competition at the 1984 Olympic Games. *Research Quarterly for Exercise and Sport, 59*, 103-107.

Whissell, R., Lyons, S., Wilkinson, D., & Whissell, C. (1993). National bias in judgments of olympic-level skating. *Perceptual and Motor Skills, 77*, 355-358.

26   Judges: Favoring Their Own

Lehman, D. R., & Reifman, A. (1987). Spectator influence on basketball officiating. *The Journal of Social Psychology, 127*, 673-675.

Mohr, P. B., & Larsen, K. (1998). Ingroup favoritism in umpiring decisions in Australian football. *The Journal of Social Psychology, 138*, 495-504.

Sumner, J., & Mobley, M. (1981, July 2). Are cricket umpires biased?*New Scientist, 91*, 29-31.

27   When to Pull the Goalie

Morrison, D. G., & Wheat, R. D. (1986). Misapplications Reviews: Pulling the goalie revisited. *Interfaces, 16*, 28-34.

Washburn, A. (1991). Still more on pulling the goalie. *Interfaces, 21*, 59-64.

28   And the Winner by a Split Decision is___.

Stallings, W. M., & Gillmore, G. M. (1972). Estimating the interjudge reliability of the Ali-Frazier fight. *Journal of Applied Psychology, 56,* 435-436.

29   Pitchers' Reputations and the Strike Zone

Rainey, D. W., & Larsen, J. D. (1988). Balls, strikes, and norms: Rule violations and normative rules among baseball umpires. *Journal of Sport & Exercise Psychology, 10,* 75-80.

Rainey, D. W., Larsen, J. D., & Stephenson, A. (1989). The effects of a pitcher's reputation on umpires' calls of balls and strikes. *Journal of Sport Behavior, 12,* 139-150.

30   Out at First...Well, Not Necessarily

Brinkman, J., & Euchner, C. (1987). *The Umpire's Handbook* (rev. ed.). Lexington, MA: Stephen Greene Press.

Larsen, J. D., & Rainey, D. W. (1991). Judgment bias in baseball umpires' first base calls: A computer simulation. *Journal of Sport & Exercise Psychology, 13,* 75-79.

31   The View from the Dugout

Lindsey, G. R. (1963). An investigation of strategies in baseball. *Operations Research, 11,* 477-501.

32   Two Minutes Roughing... Make That Boarding

Vokey, J. R., & Russell, G. W. (2001). *On the structure of sports penalties as measures of aggression: Is ice hockey a unidimensional sport?* Unpublished manuscript. University of Lethbridge.

VI. MYTHS SURROUNDING SPORTS

33   Abner Doubleday and Cooperstown

Gould., S. J. (1991). *Bully for Brontosaurus.* New York: W. W. Norton & Co.

34   Brainstorming: Are Two Heads Better Than One?

Osborn, A. F. (1957). *Applied imagination* (rev. ed.). New York: Scribner's.

Stroebe, W., Diehl, M., & Abakoumkin, G. (1992). The illusion of group effectivity. *Personality and Social Psychology Bulletin, 18,* 643-650.

35   That Ol' Devil Moon

Russell, G. W., & deGraaf, J. (1985). Lunar cycles and human aggression: A replication. Social *Behavior and Personality, 13,* 143-146.

Russell, G. W., & Dua, M. (1983). Lunar influences on human aggression. *Social Behavior and Personality, 11,* 41-44.

* Amaddeo, F., Bisoffi, G., Micciolo, R.,Piccinelli, M., & Tansella, M. (1997). Frequency of contact with community-based psychiatric services and the lunar cycle: A 10-year case-register study. *Social Psychiatry and Psychiatric Epidemiology, 32,* 323-326.

* Kelly, I. W., & Martens, R. (1994). Geophysical variables and behavior: LXXVIII. Lunar phase and birthrate: An update. *Psychological Reports, 75,* 507-511.

36 The Mars Effect

Eysenck, H. J., & Nias, D. K. B. (1982). *Astrology: Science or superstition?* New York: St. Martin's Press.

Gauquelin, M., & Gauquelin, F. (1979-80, Winter). Star U.S. sportsmen display the Mars effect. *Skeptical Inquirer, 4,* 31-43.

Kelly, I. W., & Saklofske, D. H. (1994). Psychology and pseudoscience. *Encyclopedia of Human Behavior Vol. 3.* (pp. 611-618). New York: Academic Press.

Nienhuys, J. W. (1993). Dutch investigations of the Gauquelin Mars Effect. *Journal of Scientific Exploration, 7,* 231-292.

37 We All Have our Ups and Downs

Bainbridge, W. (1978). Biorhytms: Evaluating a pseudoscience. *Skeptical Inquirer, 2,* 40-56.

Baron, R. A., Russell, G. W., & Arms, R. L. (1985). Negative ions and behavior: Impact on mood, memory, and aggression among Type A and Type B persons. *Journal of Personality and Social Psychology, 48,* 746-754.

Fix, A. J. (1976). Biothythms and sports performance. *The Zetetic, 1,* 53-57.

Hines, T. M. (1979). Biorhythm theory: A critical review. *Skeptical Inquirer, 3,* 26-36.

Holmes, D. S., Curtright, C. A., McCaul, K. D., & Thissen, D. (1980). Bio rhythms: Their utility for predicting postoperative recuperative time, death, and athletic performance. *Journal of Applied Psychology, 65,* 233-236.

Louis, A. M. (1978, April). Should you buy biorhythms? *Psychology Today,* 93-96.

* Hines, T. (1988). *Pseudoscience and the paranormal.* Buffalo, NY: Prometheus Books.

38 Hi There! What's Your Blood Type?

Cattell, R. B., Boutourline Young, H., & Hundleby, J. B. (1964). Blood groups and personality traits. *American Journal of Human Genetics, 16,* 397-402.

Coscarelli, W. C., Stepp, S. L., & Lyeria, R. (1989). Relationship of blood type with decision-making style and personality type. *Mankind Quarterly, 29,* 307-327.

Russell, G. W., & Ohmura, M. (2001). *Blood types and athletic performance.* Manuscript submitted for publication.

Sullivan, K. (1996, January 1). A or B? B or AB? In Japan, blood type is the be all and end all. *International Herald Tribune,* pp. 1, 5.

39   Not Tonight Dear, the Big Game is Tomorrow

Anshel, M. H. (1981). Effects of sexual activity on athletic performance. *The Physician and Sportsmedicine, 9,* 64-68.

Boone, T., & Gilmore, S. (1995). Effects of sexual intercourse on maximal aerobic power, oxygen pulse, and double product in male sedentary subjects. *Journal of Sports Medicine and Physical Fitness, 35,* 214-217.

Butt, D. S. (1990). The sexual response as exercise: A brief review and theoretical proposal. *Sports Medicine, 9,* 330-343.

Eysenck, H. J., Nias, D. K. B., & Cox, D. N. (1982). Sport and personality. *Advances in Behavior Research and Therapy, 4,* 1-56.

No sex until after World Cup qualifying games. (1997, March 14). *USA Today,* p. 2B.

VII. NEAR MYTHS

40   Sport Widows

Gantz, W., Wenner, L. A., Carrico, C., & Knorr, M. (1995). Televised sports and marital relationships. *Sociology of Sport Journal, 12,* 306-323.

Russell, G. W., & Arms, R. L. (2001). *Sports widows.* [Unpublished raw data].

41   Pitching Illusions

Bahill, A. T., & Karnavas, W. J. (1993). The perceptual illusion of baseball's rising fastball and breaking curveball. *Journal of Experimental Psychology: Human Perception and Performance, 18,* 3-14.

McBeath, M. K. (1990). The rising fastball: Baseball's impossible pitch. *Perception, 19,* 545-552.

42   Batting Under Pressure

Davis, M. H., & Harvey, J. C. (1992). Declines in major league batting performance as a function of game pressure: A drive theory analysis. *Journal of Applied Social Psychology, 22,* 714-735.

4 3   When You're Hot, You're Not

Gilovich, T., Vallone, R., & Tversky, A. (1985). The hot hand in basketball: On the misperception of random sequences. *Cognitive Psychology, 17,* 295-314.

*   Gilden, D. L., & Gray Wilson, S. (1995). Streaks in skilled performance. *Psychonomic Bulletin & Review, 2,* 260-265.

4 4   Momentum: On a Roll or Not?

Vergin, R. C. (2000). Winning streaks in sports and the misperception of momentum. *Journal of Sport Behavior, 23,* 181-197.

4 5   Icing the Shooter

Kozar, B., Vaughn, R. E., Whitfield, K. E., & Lord, R. H. (1994). Importance of free-throws at various stages of basketball games. *Perceptual and Motor Skills, 78,* 243-248.

Kozar, B., Whitfield, K. E., Lord, R. H., & Mechikoff, R. A. (1993). Timeouts before free-throws: Do the statistics support the strategy? *Perceptual and Motor Skills, 76,* 47-50.

4 6   Jockeys, Gender and Dollars

Grimes, P. W., & Ray, M. A. (1995). Career winnings and gender in thoroughbred racing. *Sociology of Sport Journal, 12,* 96-104.

McCombes, M. E., & Sommers, P. M. (1983). Are women the weaker sex in Grand Prix jumping? The answer is nay. *Journal of Recreational Mathematics, 15,* 161-167.

Ray, M. A., & Grimes, P. W. (1993). Jockeying for position: Winnings and gender discrimination on the thoroughbred track. *Social Science Quarterly, 74,* 46-61.

4 7   NFL Myths

Onwuegbuzie, A. J. (1999). Defense or offense? Which is the better predictor of success for professional football teams? *Perceptual and Motor Skills, 89,* 151-159.

Onwuegbuzie, A. J. (2000). Is defense or offense more important for professional football teams? A replication study using data from the 1998-1999 regular football season. *Perceptual and Motor Skills, 90,* 640-648.

Young, T. J., & French, L. A. (1995). Myths and legends of the National Football League: The function of folklore in sports. *Psychology: A Journal of Human Behavior, 32,* 25-26.

4 8   Morality on the Links

Erffmeyer, E. S. (1984). Rule-violating behavior on the golf course. *Perceptual and Motor Skills, 59,* 591-596.

Sommers, R. T. (1995). *Golf anecdotes.* New York: Oxford University Press.

VIII. SPORTS HEROES AND RECORDS

4 9   Sport Heroes as Agents of Change

Kalichman, S. C., Russell, R. L., Hunter, T. L., & Sarwer, D. B. (1993). Ervin "Magic" Johnson's serostatus disclosure: Effects of men's perceptions of AIDS. *Journal of Consulting and Clinical Psychology, 61,* 887-891.

Penner, L. A., & Fritzsche, B. A. (1993). Magic Johnson and reactions to people with AIDS: A natural experiment. *Journal of Applied Social Psychology, 23,* 1035-1050.

Ohanian, R. (1991). The impact of celebrity spokespersons' perceived image on consumers' intention to purchase. *Journal of Advertising Research, 31,* 46-54.

Smith, T. W. (1986). The polls: The most admired man and woman. *Public Opinion Quarterly, 50,* 573-583.

Sumser, J. (1992). Campus knowledge of AIDS before and after "Magic" Johnson announced his infection. *Social Science Research, 76,* 182-184.

Zimet, G. D., Lazebnik, R., DiClemente, R. J., Anglin, T. M., Williams, P., & Ellick, E. M. (1993). The relationship of Magic Johnson's announcement of HIV infection to the AIDS attitudes of Junior high school students. *The Journal of Sex Research, 30,* 129-134.

5 0   The O.J. Simpson Verdict

CNN/USA *Today*/Gallup Poll. (1995, October 3) *USA Today.*

Nier, J. A., Mottola, G. R., & Gaertner, S. L. (2000). The O.J. Simpson criminal verdict as a racially symbolic event: A longitudinal analysis of racial attitude change. *Personality and Social Psychology Bulletin, 26,* 507-516.

Sachs, C. J., Peek, C. P., Baraff, L. J., & Hasselblad, V. (1998). Failure of the mandatory domestic violence reporting law to increase medical facility referral to police. *Annals of Emergency Medicine, 31,* 488-494.

* Murray, C. B., Kaiser, R., & Taylor, S. (1997). The O.J. Simpson verdict: Predictors of beliefs about innocence or guilt. *Journal of Social Issues, 53,* 455-476.

5 1   What Trading Cards Can Tell Us

Gill, A. M., & Brajer, V. (1994). Baseball stars and baseball cards: A new look at monopsony in major league baseball. *Social Science Quarterly, 7,* 195-203.

Hanssen, A., & Anderson, T. (1999). Has discrimination lessened over time? A test using baseball's star vote. *Economic Inquiry, 37,* 326-327.

Nardinelli, C., & Simon, C. (1990). Customer racial discrimination in the market for memorabilia: The case of baseball. *The Quarterly Journal of Economics, 105,* 575-595.

52   A Measure of Sport Greatness

Golden, B. L., & Wasil, E. A. (1987). Ranking outstanding sports records. *Interfaces, 17,* 32-42.

53   How Great Thou Art

Pankin, M. D. (1978). Evaluating offensive performance in baseball. *Operations Research, 26,* 610-619.

*   Cover, T. M., & Keilers, C. W. (1977). An offensive earned-run average for baseball. *Operations Research, 25,* 729-740.

54   A Record Among Records

Gould, S. J. (1991). *Bully for brontosaurus.* New York: W. W. Norton & Co.

55   Pros and Cons

Benedict, J., & Yaeger, D. (1998). *Pros and cons: The criminals who play in the NFL.* New York: Warner Books.

Eastman, S. T., & Riggs, K. E. (1994). Televised sports and ritual: Fan experiences. *Sociology of Sport Journal, 11,* 249-274.

Wahl, G., & Wertheim, L. J. (1998). Paternity ward. *Sports Illustrated,* May 4, pp. 62-71.

IX.   THE SPORTING ENVIRONMENT

56   Weather and Baseball

Adair, R. K. (1990). *The physics of baseball.* New York: Harper Row.

Adair, R. K. (1995, May). The physics of baseball. *Physics Today,* 26-31.

57   Hot Players, Hot Tempers

Reifman, A. S., Larrick, R. P., & Fein, S. (1991). Temper and temperature on the diamond: The heat-aggression relationship in major league baseball. *Personality and Social Psychology Bulletin, 17,* 580-585.

58   Playing Under the Dome

Horn, J. C. (1988). Dome-inating the game. *Sporting Life, 22.*

Zeller, R. A., & Jurkovac, T. (1989). A dome stadium: Does it help the home team in the National Football League? *Sport Place, 3,* 37-39.

Zeller, R. A., & Jurkovac, T. (1989). Doming the stadium: The case for baseball. *Sport Place, 3,* 35-38.

5 9   Putting Sports on a Firm Footing

Goodman, G. H., & McAndrew, F. T. (1993). Domes and astroturf: A note on the relationship between the physical environment and the performance of major league baseball players. *Environment and Behavior, 25,* 121-125.

McCarthy, P. (1989). Artificial turf: Does it cause more injuries? *The Physician and Sportsmedicine, 17,* 159-161, 164.

6 0   Litterbugs and Litterbags

Baltes, M. M., & Hayward, S. C. (1976). Application and evaluation of strategies to reduce pollution: Behavioral control of littering in a football stadium. *Journal of Applied Psychology, 61,* 501-506.

X. RISKS, HEALTH, AND SPORTS

6 1   Exercise, Hostility and Life Expectancy

Barefoot, J. C., Dahlstrom, W. G., & Williams, R. B. (1983). Hostility, CHD incidence, and total mortality: A 25-year follow-up study of 255 physicians. *Psychosomatic Medicine, 45,* 59-63.

Paffenbarger, Jr., R. S., Hyde, R. T., Wing, A. L., & Hsieh, C. (1986). Physical activity, all-cause mortality, and longevity of college alumni. *New England Journal of Medicine, 314,* 605-613.

Polednak, A. P., & Damon, A. (1970). College athletics, longevity, and cause of death. *Human Biology, 42,* 28-46.

6 2   Do Right-handers Outlive Southpaws?

Aggleton, J. P., Kentridge, R. W., & Neave, N. J. (1993). Evidence for longevity differences between left handed and right handed men: An archival study of cricketers. *Journal of Epidemiology and Community Health, 47,* 206-209.

Coren, S., & Halpern, D. F. (1991). Left-handedness: A marker for decreased survival fitness. *Psychological Bulletin, 109,* 90-106.

Halpern, D. F., & Coren, S. (1993). Left-handedness and life span: A reply to Harris. *Psychological Bulletin, 114,* 235-241.

Harris, L. J. (1993). Do left-handers die sooner than right-handers? Commentary on Coren and Halpern's (1991) "Left-handedness: A marker for decreased survival fitness". *Psychological Bulletin, 114,* 203-234.

6 3 The Silent Epidemic: Boxing's Dark Side

Barth, J. T. et al. (1989). Mild head injury in sports: Neuropsychological sequelae and recovery of function. In H. S. Levin, H. M. Eisenberg & A. L. Benton (Eds.), *Mild head injury* (pp. 257-275). New York: Oxford University Press.

Casson, I. R., Sham, R., Campbell, E. A., Tarlau, M., & DiDomenico, A. (1982). Neurological and CT evaluation of knocked-out boxers. *Journal of Neurology, Neurosurgery, and Psychiatry, 45,* 170-174.

Enk, I., Matser, J. T., Kessels, A. G., Lezak, M. D., Jordan, B. D., & Troost, J. (1999). Neuropsychological impairment in amateur soccer players. *Journal of the American Medical Association, 282,* 971-973.

Ex-boxers face Alzheimer risk, study finds. (1989), April 17). *The Toronto Star,* p. A19.

Levin, H. S., Eisenberg, H. M., & Benton, A. L. (Eds.).(1989). *Mild head injury.* New York: Oxford University Press.

6 4 Keeping your Ball on the Fairway

Standaert, S. M. et al. (1995). Enrlichiosis in a golf-oriented retirement community. *The New England Journal of Medicine, 333,* 420-425.

6 5 Designated Spitters

Greene, J. C., Walsh, M. M., & Letendre, M. A. (1998). Prevalence of spit tobacco use across studies of professional baseball players. *Journal of the California Dental Association, 26,* 358-364.

Walsh, M. M., Hilton, J. F., Ernster, V. L., Masouredis, C. M., & Grady, D. G. (1994). Prevalence, patterns, and correlates of spit tobacco use in a college athlete population. *Addictive Behavior, 19,* 411-427.

Wann, D. L. (1998). Tobacco use and sport fandom. *Perceptual and Motor Skills, 86,* 878.

Wann, D. L. (1998). A preliminary investigation of the relationship between alcohol use and sport fandom. *Social Behavior and Personality, 26,* 287-290

6 6 Referees, Umpires and Stress

Rainey, D. (1995). Sources of stress among baseball and softball umpires. *Journal of Applied Sport Psychology, 7,* 1-10.

6 7 Warmups: A Bit of a Stretch

Pope, R. P., Herbert, R. D., & Kirwan, J. D. (1998). Effects of ankle dorsiflexion range and pre-exercise calf muscle stretching on injury risk in Army recruits. *Australian Journal of Physiotherapy, 44,* 165-172.

Pope, R. P., Herbert, R. D., Kirwan J. D., & Graham, B. J. (2000). A randomized trial of preexercise stretching for prevention of lower-limb injury. *Medicine & Science in Sports & Exercise, 32,* 271-277.

XI. MEDIA AND THE BUSINESS OF SPORTS

68   Sport Preferences on Television
Bibby, R. W. (1995). *The Bibby report: Social trends Canadian style.* Toronto: Stoddart.
Wenner, L. A., & Gantz, W. (1989). The audience experience with sports on television. In L. A. Wenner (Ed.), *Media, sports, and society* (pp. 241-269). Newbury Park: CA: Sage.

69   Does Televising College Football Hurt Attendance?
Fizel, J. L., & Bennett, R. W. (1989). The impact of college football telecasts on college football attendance. *Social Science Quarterly, 70,* 980-988.
Kaempfer, W. H., & Pacey, P. L. (1986). Televising college football: The complementarity of attendance and viewing. *Social Science Quarterly, 67,* 176-185.

70   Predicting College Team Standings
Blumenfield, W. S. (1985). Ability of *Sports Illustrated* to predict 10 college football conference standings. *Perceptual and Motor Skills, 61,* 1004.
Showalter, S. W. (1985). Sports polls: Predictive or promotional? *Journalism Quarterly, 20,* 100-104.

71   Race and Attendance
Brown, R. W., & Jewell, R. T. (1994). Is there customer discrimination in college basketball? The premium fans pay for white players. *Social Science Quarterly, 75,* 401-413.
Burdekin, R. C. K., & Idson, T. L. (1991). Customer preferences, attendance and the racial structure of professional basketball teams. *Applied Economics, 23,* 179-186.
Schollaert, P. T., & Smith, D. H. (1987). Team racial composition and sports attendance. *Sociological Quarterly, 28,* 71-87.
Timmerman, T. A. (2000). Racial diversity, age diversity, interdependence, and team performance. *Small Group Research, 31,* 592-606.

72   Win One for the Giver
Brooker, G., & Klastorin, T. D. (1981). To the victors belong the spoils? College athletics and alumni giving. *Social Science Quarterly, 62,* 744-750.
Gaski, J. F., & Etzel, M. J. (1984). Collegiate athletic success and alumni generosity: Dispelling the myth. *Social Behavior and Personality, 12,* 29-

38.

Sigelman, L., & Carter, R. (1979). Win one for the giver? Alumni giving and big-time college sports. *Social Science Quarterly, 60,* 284-294.

Wann, D. L., & Somerville, D. J. (2000). The relationship between university team identification and alumni contributions. *International Sports Journal, Winter,* 138-144.

7 3   Snippets from the Indy 500

Edgley, C. (1987). Beer, speed, and real men: Indianapolis during the month of May. *Sport Place, 1,* 20-26.

Russell, G. W. (1993). *The social psychology of sport.* New York: Springer-Verlag.

7 4   Sex Sells, How about Violence?

Jones, J. C. H., Ferguson, D. G., & Stewart, K. G. (1993). Blood sports and cherry pie: Some economics of violence in the National Hockey League. *American Journal of Economics and Sociology, 52,* 63-78.

Jones, J. C. H., Stewart, K. G., & Sunderman, R. (1996). From the arena into the streets: Hockey violence, economic incentives and public policy. *American Journal of Economics and Sociology, 55,* 231-243.

Russell, G. W. (1986). Does sports violence increase box office receipts? *International Journal of Sports Psychology, 17,* 173-183.

7 5   Sex, Violence and Videogames

Anderson, C. A., & Ford, C. M. (1986). Affect of the game player: Short-term effects of highly and mildly aggressive video games. *Personality and Social Psychology Bulletin, 12,* 390-402.

Ballard, M. E., & Wiest, J. R. (1996). Mortal Kombat (tm): The effects of violent videogame play on males' hostility and cardiovascular responding. *Journal of Applied Social Psychology, 26,* 717-730.

Goldstein, J. H. (1998). Immortal kombat: War toys and violent video games. In J. H. Goldstein (Ed.), *Why we watch: The attractions of violent entertainment* (pp. 53-68). New York: Oxford University Press.

XII. THE FACE OF VIOLENCE: SOME NEW WRINKLES

7 6   Letting Off Steam: Does it Help?

Bushman, B. J., Baumeister, R. F., & Stack, A. D. (1999). Catharsis, aggression, and persuasive influence: Self-fulfilling or self-defeating prophecies? *Journal of Personality and Social Psychology, 76,* 367-376.

Pennebaker, J. W., Hughes, C. F., & O'Heeron, R. C. (1987). The psychophysiology of confession: Linking inhibitory and psychosomatic processes. *Journal of Personality and Social Psychology, 52,* 781-793.

Russell, G. W. (1981). Spectator moods at an aggressive sports event. *Journal of Sport Psychology, 3,* 217-227.

Russell, G. W. (1993). *The social psychology of sport.* New York: Plenum.

Russell, G. W. (1993). Violent sports entertainment and the promise of catharsis. *Medienpsychologie, 2,* 101-105.

Russell, G. W., Di Lullo, S. L., & Di Lullo, D. (1988-89). Effects of observing competitive and violent versions of a sport. *Current Psychology: Research & Reviews, 7,* 312-321.

7 7   An Exception of Sorts

Nosanchuk, T.A., & MacNeil, M. L. C. (1989). Examination of the effects of traditional and modern martial arts training on aggressiveness. *Aggressive Behavior, 15,* 153-159.

Trulson, M. E. (1986). Martial arts training: A novel "cure" for juvenile delinquency. *Human Relations, 39,* 1131-1140.

7 8   A History of Hockey Violence

Russell, G. W. (1993). *The social psychology of sport.* New York: Springer-Verlag.

7 9   Violence: A Winning or Losing Strategy?

Engelhardt, G. M. (1995). Fighting behavior and winning National Hockey League games: A paradox. *Perceptual and Motor Skills, 80,* 416-418.

McCaw, S. T., & Walker, J. D. (1999). Winning the Stanley Cup final series is related to incurring fewer penalties for violent behavior. *Texas Medicine, 85,* 66-69.

8 0   Interracial Aggression: Between the Mound and the Plate

Goff, B. L., Shughart, W. F., & Tollison, R. D. (1997). Batter up! Moral hazard and the effects of the designated hitter rule on hit batsmen. *Economic Inquiry, 35,* 555-561.

Timmerman, T. A. (in press). Violence and race in professional baseball: Getting better or getting worse? *Aggressive Behavior.*

8 1   Some Uniform Results

Frank, M. G., & Gilovich, T. (1988). The dark side of self-and social perception: Black uniforms and aggression in professional sports. *Journal of Personality*

and Social Psychology, 54, 74-85.
Zimbardo, P. G. (1970). The human choice: Individuation, reason, and order versus deindividuation, impulse, and chaos. In W. J. Arnold & D. Levine (Eds.), *Nebraska symposium on motivation, 1969,* Lincoln: University of Nebraska Press.

8 2   Goons, Enforcers and the Power of Obedience

Hofling, C. K., Brotzman, E., Dalrymple, S., Graves, N., & Pierce, C. M. (1966). An experimental study in nurse-physician relationships. *Journal of Nervous and Mental Diseases, 143,* 171-180.
Milgram, S. (1974). *Obedience to authority.* New York: Cambridge University Press.

8 3   "Why Me.........Why MEeeeeeeeeeeeeeee?"

Kenrick, D. T., & Sheets, V. (1993). Homicidal fantasies. *Ecology and Sociobiology, 14,* 231-246.
Russell, G. W., & Baenninger, R. (1996). Murder most foul: Predictors of an affirmative response to an outrageous question. *Aggressive Behavior, 22,* 175-181.
Wann, D. L., Peterson, R. R., Cothran, C., & Dykes, M. (1999). Sport fan aggression and anonymity: The importance of team identification. *Social Behavior and Personality, 27,* 597-602.

8 4   Boxing, Football and Homicide

Miller, T. Q., Heath, L., & Molcan, J. R. (1991). Imitative violence in the real world: A reanalysis of homicide rates following championship prize fights. *Aggressive Behavior, 17,* 121-134.
Phillips, D. P. (1983). The impact of mass media violence on U.S. homicides. *American Sociological Review, 48,* 560-568.
White, G. F. (1989). Media and violence: The case of professional championship games. *Aggressive Behavior, 15,* 423-433.

8 5   The Long Arm of Sport Violence

Drake, B., & Pandey, S. (1996). Do child abuse rates increase on those days on which professional sporting events are held? *Journal of Family Violence, 11,* 205-218.
Sachs, C. J., & Chu, L. D. (2000). The association between professional football games and domestic violence in Los Angeles county. *Journal of Interpersonal Violence, 15,* 1192-1201.
Tesler, B. S., & Alker, H. A. (1983). Football games: Victory, defeat, and spectators' power preferences. *Journal of Research in Personality, 17,* 72-80.
White, G. F., Katz, J., & Scarborough, K. E. (1992). The impact of

professional football games upon violent assaults on women. *Violence and Victims, 7,* 157-171.

8 6 Are Athletes More Likely to Rape?

Boeringer, S. B. (1996). Influences of fraternity membership, athletics, and male living arrangements on sexual aggression. *Violence Against Women, 2,* 134-147.

Caron, S. L., Halteman, W. A., & Stacy, C. (1997). Athletes and rape: Is there a connection? *Perceptual and Motor Skills, 85,* 1379-1393.

Crosset, T. W., Ptacek, J., McDonald, M. A., & Benedict, J. R. (1996). Male student-athletes and violence against women: A survey of campus judicial affairs offices. *Violence Against Women, 2,* 163-179.

Koss, M. P., & Gaines, J. A. (1993). The prediction of sexual aggression by alcohol use, athletic participation, and fraternity affiliation. *Journal of Interpersonal Violence, 8,* 94-108.

8 7 Booze and Unruly Fans

Jeavons, C. M., & Taylor, S. P. (1985). The control of alcohol-related aggression: Redirecting the inebriate's attention to socially approved conduct. *Aggressive Behavior, 11,* 93-101.

Taylor, S. P., & Gammon, C. B. (1976). Aggressive behavior of intoxicated subjects: The effect of third-party intervention. *Journal of Studies on Alcohol, 37,* 917-930.

Taylor, S. P., Gammon, C. B., & Capasso, D. R. (1976). Aggression as a function of the interaction of alcohol and threat. *Journal of Personality and Social Psychology, 34,* 938-941.

Wolfe, J., Martinez, R., & Scott, W. A. (1998). Baseball and beer: An analysis of alcohol consumption patterns among male spectators at major-league sporting events. *Annals of Emergency Medicine, 31,* 629-632.

* Baron, R. A., & Richardson, D. R. (1994). *Human aggression* (2nd ed.). New York: Plenum Press.

XIII. FANS

8 8 As the Team Goes, So Go its Fans

Cialdini, R. B., Borden, R. J., Thorne, A., Walker, M., Freeman, S., & Sloan, L. (1976). Basking in reflected glory: Three (football) field studies. *Journal of Personality and Social Psychology, 34,* 366-375.

Hirt, E. R., Zillmann, D., Erickson, G. A., & Kennedy, C. (1992). Costs and benefits of allegiance: Changes in fans' self-ascribed competencies after team victory versus defeat. *Journal of Personality and Social Psychology, 63,*

724-738.

Mann, L. (1974). On being a sore loser: How fans react to their team's failure. *Australian Journal of Psychology, 26,* 37-47.

Schweitzer, K., Zillmann, D., Weaver, J. B., & Luttrell, E. S. (1992). Perception of threatening events in the emotional aftermath of a televised college football game. *Journal of Broadcasting & Electronic Media, 36,* 75-82.

Wann, D. L., & Branscombe, N. R. (1990). Die-hard and fair-weather fans: Effects of identification on BIRGing and CORFing tendencies. *Journal of Sport and Social Issues, 14,* 103-117.

* Wann, D. L. (1994). Biased evaluations of highly identified sport spectators: A response to Hirt and Ryalls. *Perceptual and Motor Skills, 79,* 105- 106.

* Wann, D. l., Melnick, M. J., Russell, G. W., & Pease, D. G. (2001). *Sport fans: The psychology and social impact of spectators.* New York: Routledge.

89 Football Weekends on Campus

Coons, C. J., Howard-Hamilton, M., & Waryold, D. (1995). College sports and fan aggression: Implications for residence hall discipline. *Journal of College Student Development, 36,* 587-593.

Tesler, B. S., & Alker, H. A. (1983). Football games: Victory, defeat, and spectators' power preferences. *Journal of Research in Personality, 17,* 72-80.

90 Do Others "Do As I Do"?

Ross, L., Green, D., & House, P. (1977). The "false consensus effect": An egocentric bias in social perception and attribution processes. *Journal of Experimental Social Psychology, 13,* 279-301.

Russell, G. W., & Arms, R. L. (1998). Toward a social psychological profile of would-be rioters. *Aggressive Behavior, 24,* 219-226.

* Marks, G., & Miller, N. (1987). Ten years of research on the false-consensus effect: An empirical and theoretical review. *Psychological Bulletin, 102,* 72-90.

* Mullen, B., Atkins, J. L., Champion, D. S., Edwards, C., Hardy, D., Story, J. E., & Vanderklok, M. (1985). The false consensus effect: A meta-analysis of 115 hypothesis tests. *Journal of Experimental Social Psychology, 21,* 262-283.

91 Queue Counting

Mann, L. (1970). The social psychology of waiting lines. *American Scientist, 58,* 390-398.

Mann, L., & Taylor, K. F. (1969). Queue counting: The effect of motives upon estimates of numbers in waiting lines. *Journal of Personality and Social*

Psychology, 12, 95-103.
* Kemp, S. (1984). Estimating the sizes of sports crowds. *Perceptual and Motor Skills, 59,* 723-729.

9 2   Seeing is Believing
Adang, O. M. J. (1992, September). *Crowds, riots and the police: An observational study of collective violence.* Paper presented at the meeting of the International Society for Research on Aggression, Siena, Italy.

9 3   Who is Most Likely to Escalate a Riot?
Kerr, J. H. (1994). *Understanding soccer hooliganism.* Philadelphia: Open University Press.
Mustonen, A., Arms, R. L., & Russell, G. W. (1996). Predictors of sports spectators' proclivity for riotous behaviour in Finland and Canada. *Personality & Individual Differences, 21,* 519-525.
Russell, G. W., & Arms, R. L. (1998). Toward a social psychological profile of would-be rioters. *Aggressive Behavior, 24,* 219-226.

9 4   Calming Troubled Waters: The Peacemakers
Russell, G. W., & Arms, R. L. (in press). Calming troubled waters: Peacemakers in a sports riot. *Aggressive Behavior.*
Russell, G. W., Arms, R. L., & Mustonen, A. (1999). When cooler heads prevail: Peacemakers in a sports riot. *Scandinavian Journal of Psychology, 40,* 153-155.
Russell, G. W., & Mustonen, A. (1998). Peacemakers: Those who would intervene to quel a sports riot. *Personality & Individual Differences, 24,* 335-339.
Wann, D. L., Melnick, M. J., Russell, G. W., & Pease, D. G. (2001). *Sport fans: The psychology and social impact of spectators.* New York: Routledge.

9 5   Soccer and Politics: Latin American Bedfellows
Kapucinski, R. (1986). The soccer war. *Harpers Magazine,* June, 47-55.
Lever, J. (1969). Soccer: Opium of the Brazilian people. *Trans-action, 7,* 36-43.
* Duke, V., & Crolley, L. (1996). Football spectator behaviour in Argentina: A case of separate evolution. *The Sociological Review, 44,* 272-293.

9 6   Hooliganism in Black Africa
Amzat, L. (1983). Juju in sports - a rejoinder. *National Concord,* August 13, 23.
Doctors are not always right. (1989, November 15). *International Herald Trbune.* p. 22.
Igbinovia, P. E. (1985). Soccer hooliganism in black Africa. *International Journal of Offender Therapy and Comparative Criminology, 29,* 135-146.

XIV. TWISTS AND TURNS OF SOCIAL COGNITIONS

97 Being Happier With Less
Medvec, V. H., Madey, S. F., & Gilovich, T. (1995). When less is more: Counterfactual thinking and satisfaction among Olympic medalists. *Journal of Personality and Social Psychology, 69,* 603-610.

98 Are We Primed for Violence?
Wann, D. L., & Branscombe, N. R. (1990). Person perception when aggressive or nonaggressive sports are primed. *Aggressive Behavior, 16,* 27-32.

99 The Law of Small Numbers
Gilovitch, T. (1984). Judgmental biases in the world of sports. In W. F. Straub & J. M. Williams (eds.), *Cognitive sports psychology* (pp. 31-41). Lansing, NY: Sport Science Associates.

Tversky, A., & Kahneman, D. (1971). The belief in the "law of small numbers". *Psychological Review, 76,* 105-110.

100 Thoughts of a Racetrack Bettor
Gärling, T., Romanus, J., & Selart, M. (1994). Betting at the race track: Does risk seeking increase when losses accumulate? *Perceptual and Motor Skills, 78,* 1248-1250.

Knox, R. E., & Inkster, J. A. (1968). Postdecision dissonance at post time. *Journal of Personality and Social Psychology, 8,* 319-323.

101 Cause and Effect: What Really Causes What?
Gilovitch, T. (1984). Judgmental biases in the world of sports. In W. F. Straub & J. M. Williams (eds.), *Cognitive sports psychology* (pp. 31-41). Lansing, NY: Sport Science Associates.

102 The Sophomore Jinx
Gilovitch, T. (1984). Biased evaluations and persistence in gambling. *Journal of Personality and Social Psychology, 44,* 1110-1126.

Gilovitch, T. (1984). Judgmental biases in the world of sports. In W. F. Straub & J. M. Williams (eds.), *Cognitive sports psychology* (pp. 31-41). Lansing, NY: Sport Science Associates.

Taylor, J., & Cuave, K. L. (1994). The sophomore slump among professional baseball players: Real or imagined? *International Journal of Sport Psychology, 25,* 230-239.

103 Mind Games: Sandbagging and Self-handicapping

Gibson, B., & Sachau, D. (2000). Sandbagging as a self-presentational strategy: Claiming to be less than you are. *Personality and Social Psychology Bulletin, 26,* 56-70.

Hoffer, R. (1993, October 11). Poor Lou. *Sports Illustrated, 79,* (15), 84-86.

Jones, E. E., & Berglas, S. (1978). Control of attributions about the self through self-handicapping strategies: The appeal of alcohol and the role of underachievement. *Personality and Social Psychology Bulletin, 4,* 200-206.

Rhodewalt, F., Saltzman, A. T., & Wittmer, J. (1984). Self-handicapping among competitive athletes: The role of practice in self-esteem protection. *Basic and Applied Social Psychology, 5,* 197-209.

* Schlenker. B. R., Pontari, B. A., & Christopher, A. N. (2001). Excuses and character: Personal and social implications of excuses. *Personality and Social Psychology Review, 5,* 15-32.

ISBN 1552126382

9 781552 126387